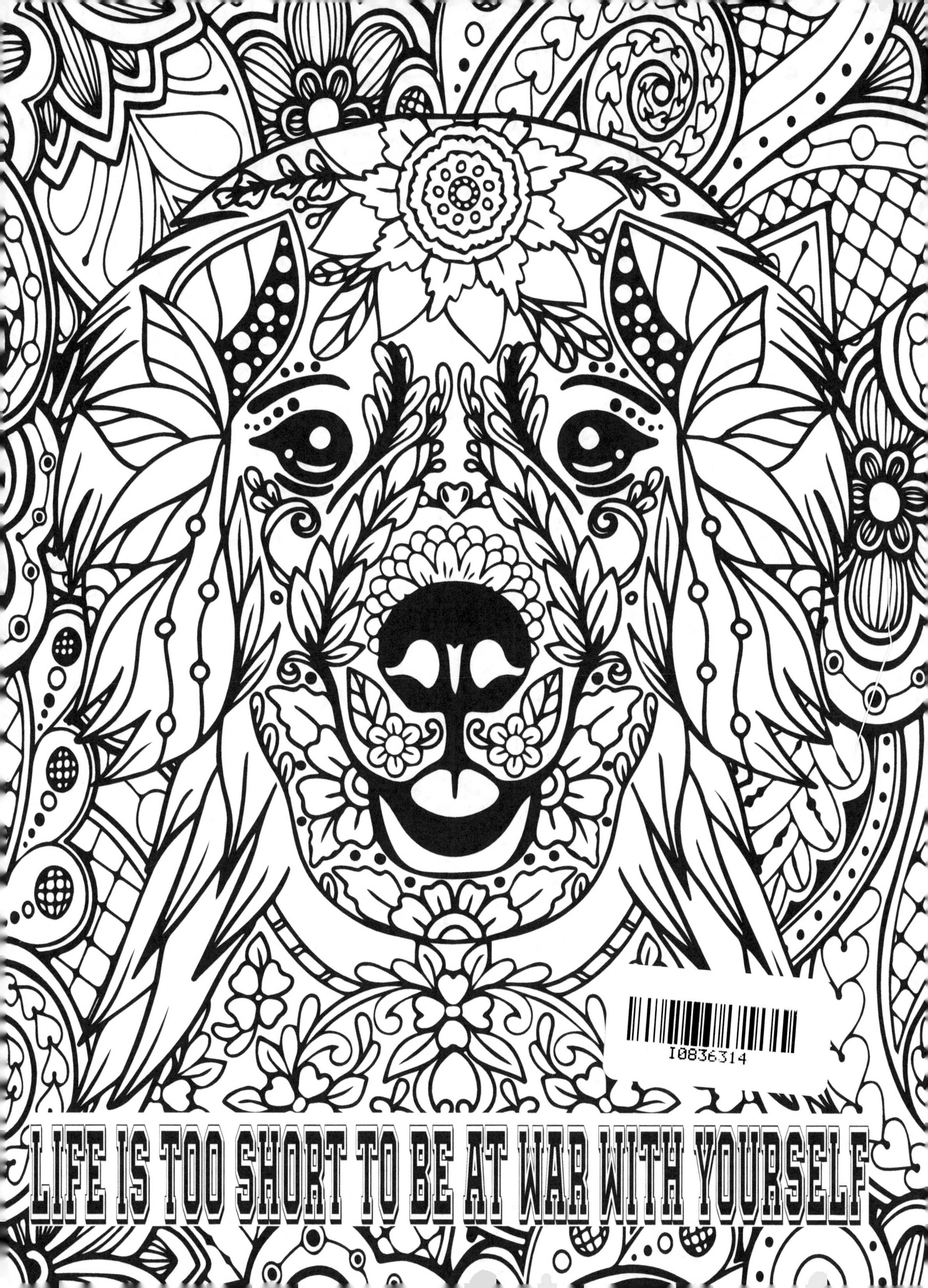
I0836314
LIFE IS TOO SHORT TO BE AT WAR WITH YOURSELF

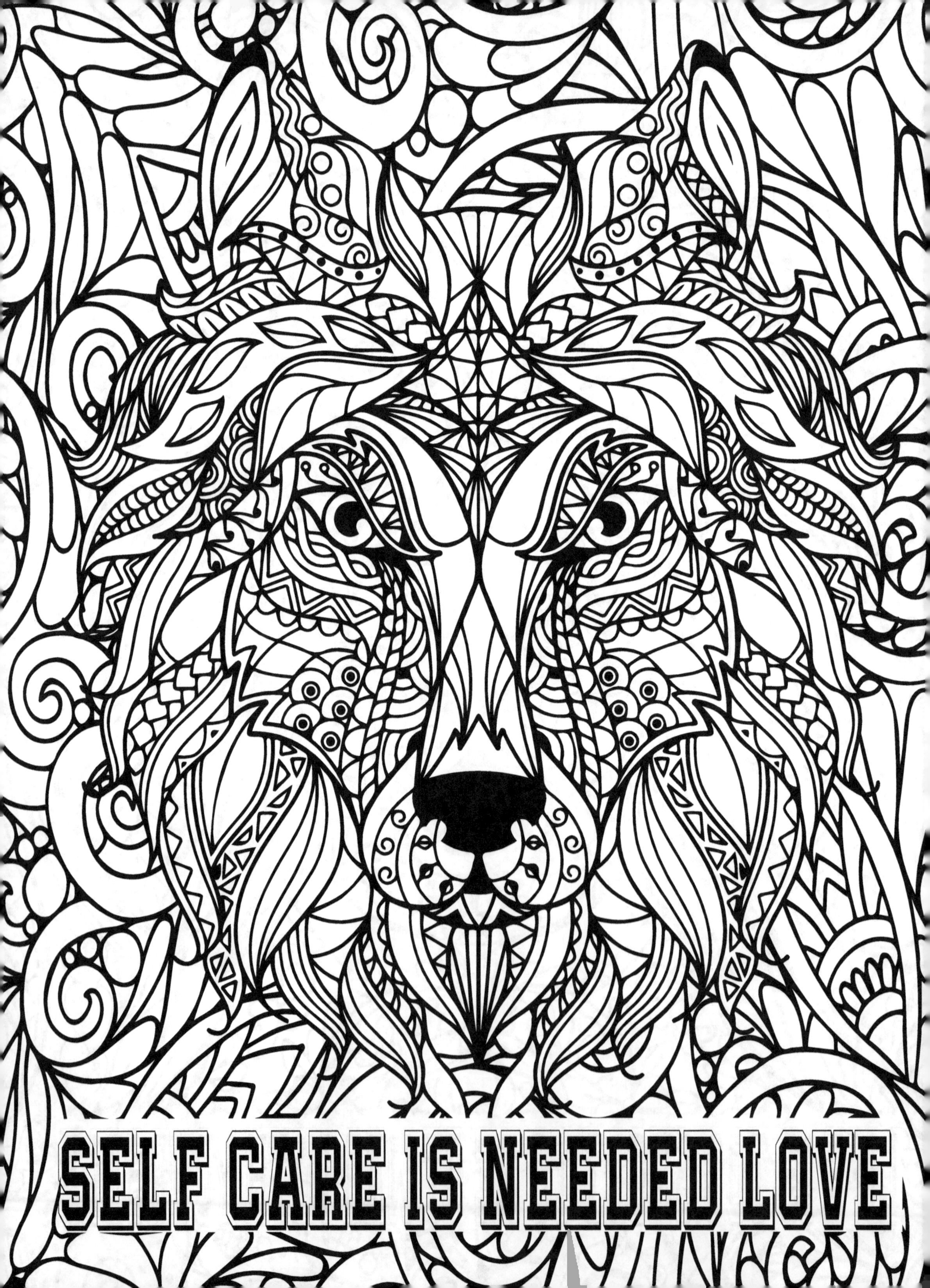
SELF CARE IS NEEDED LOVE

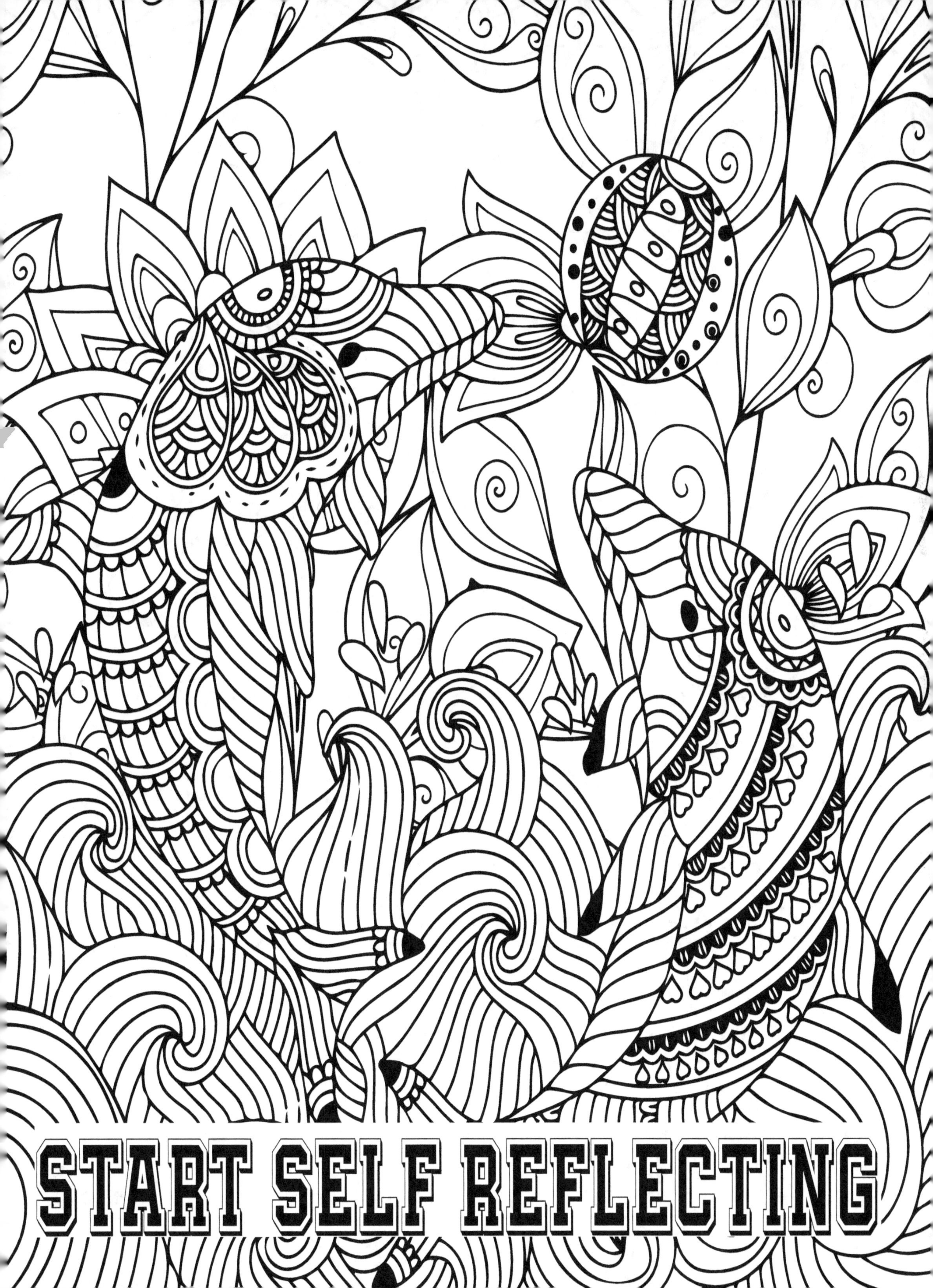
START SELF REFLECTING

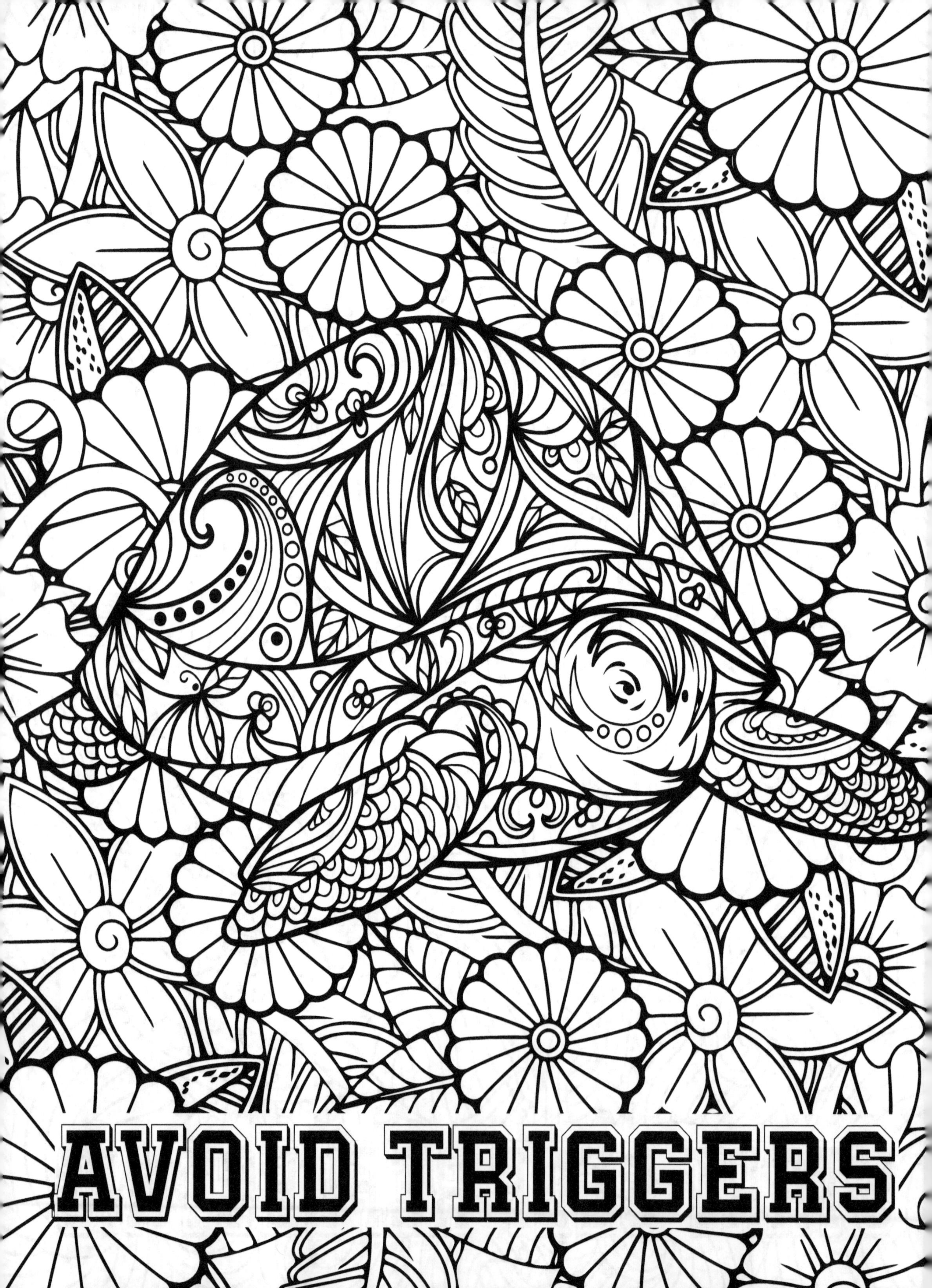
AVOID TRIGGERS

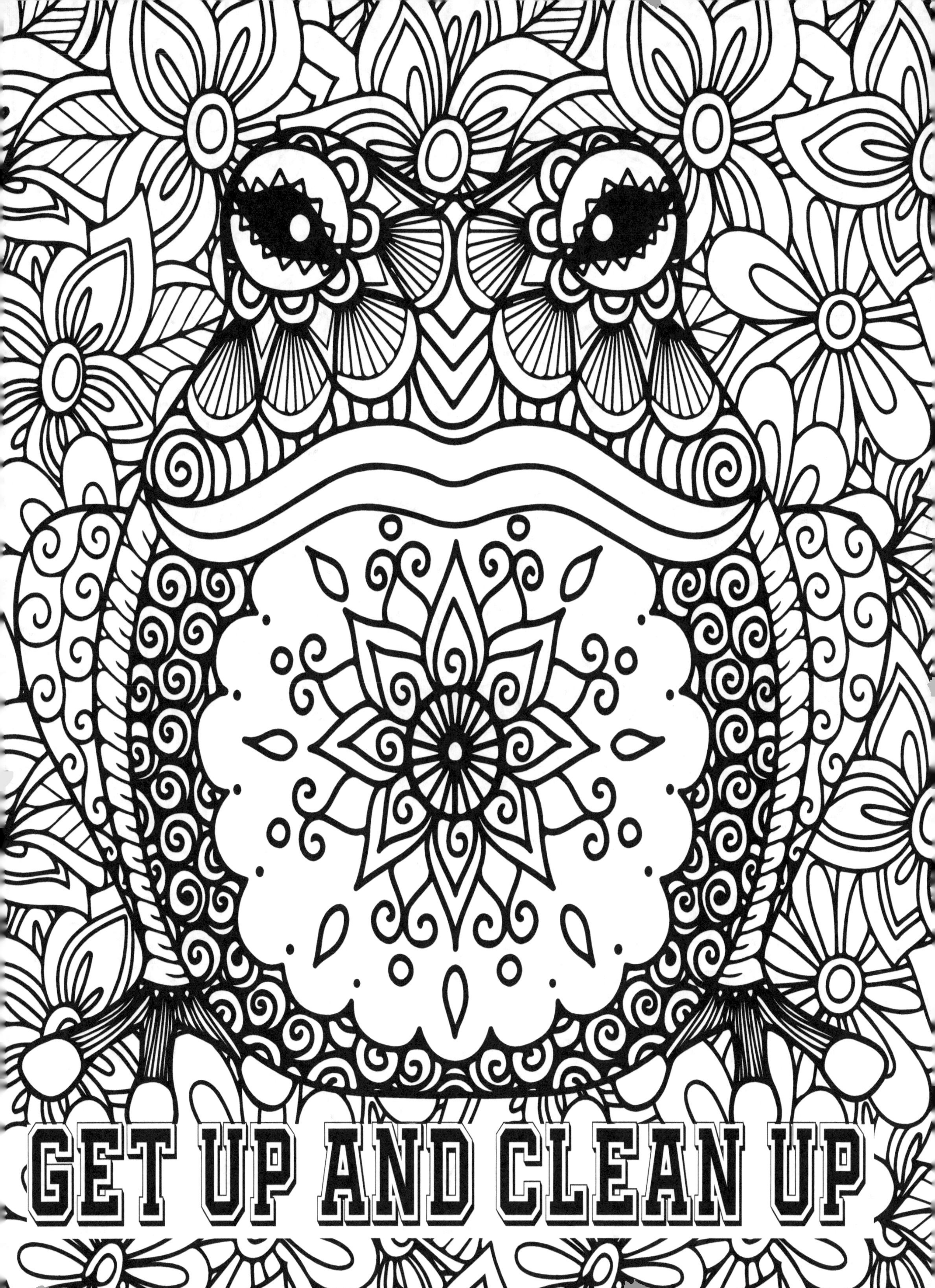
GET UP AND CLEAN UP

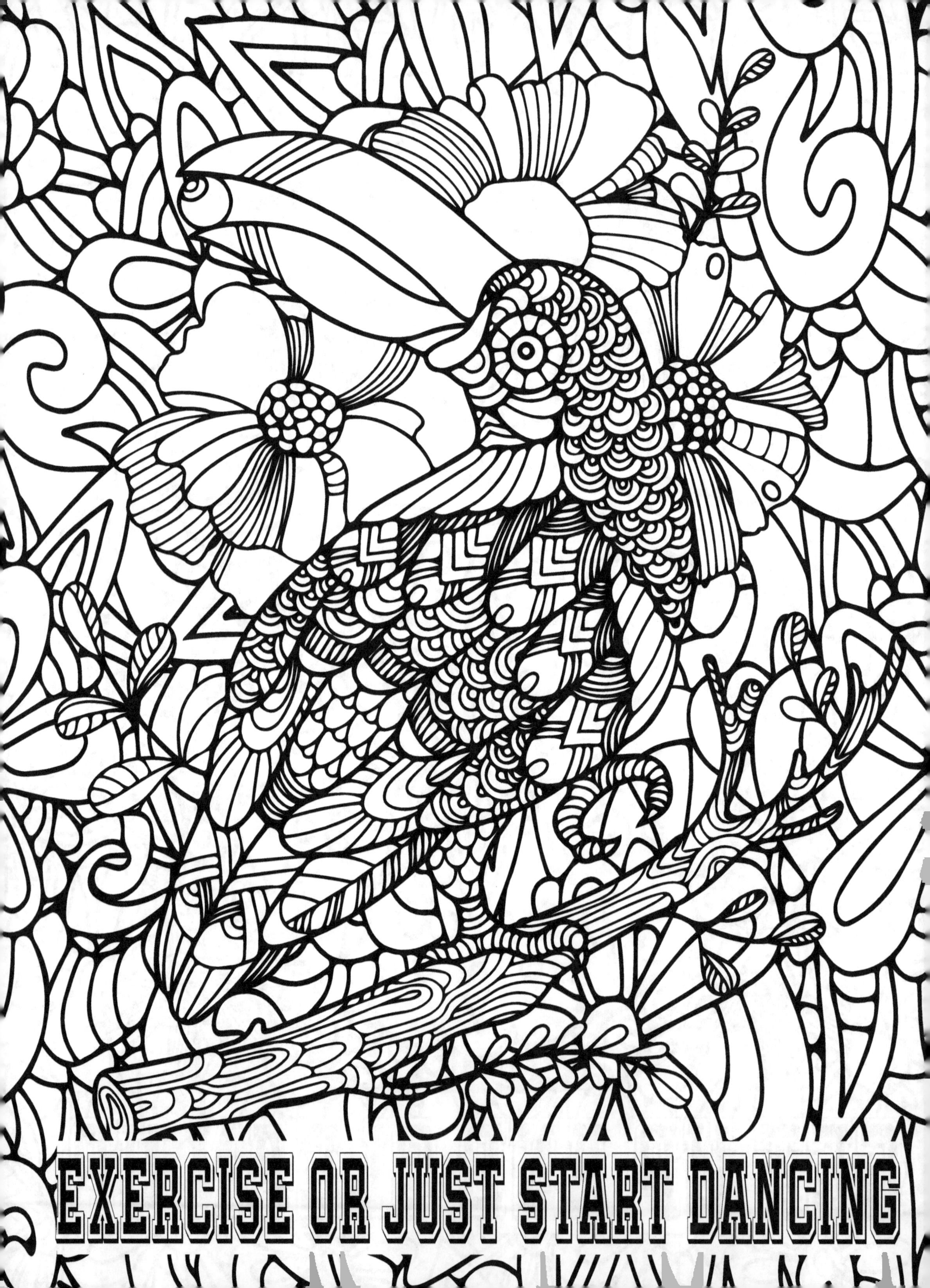
EXERCISE OR JUST START DANCING

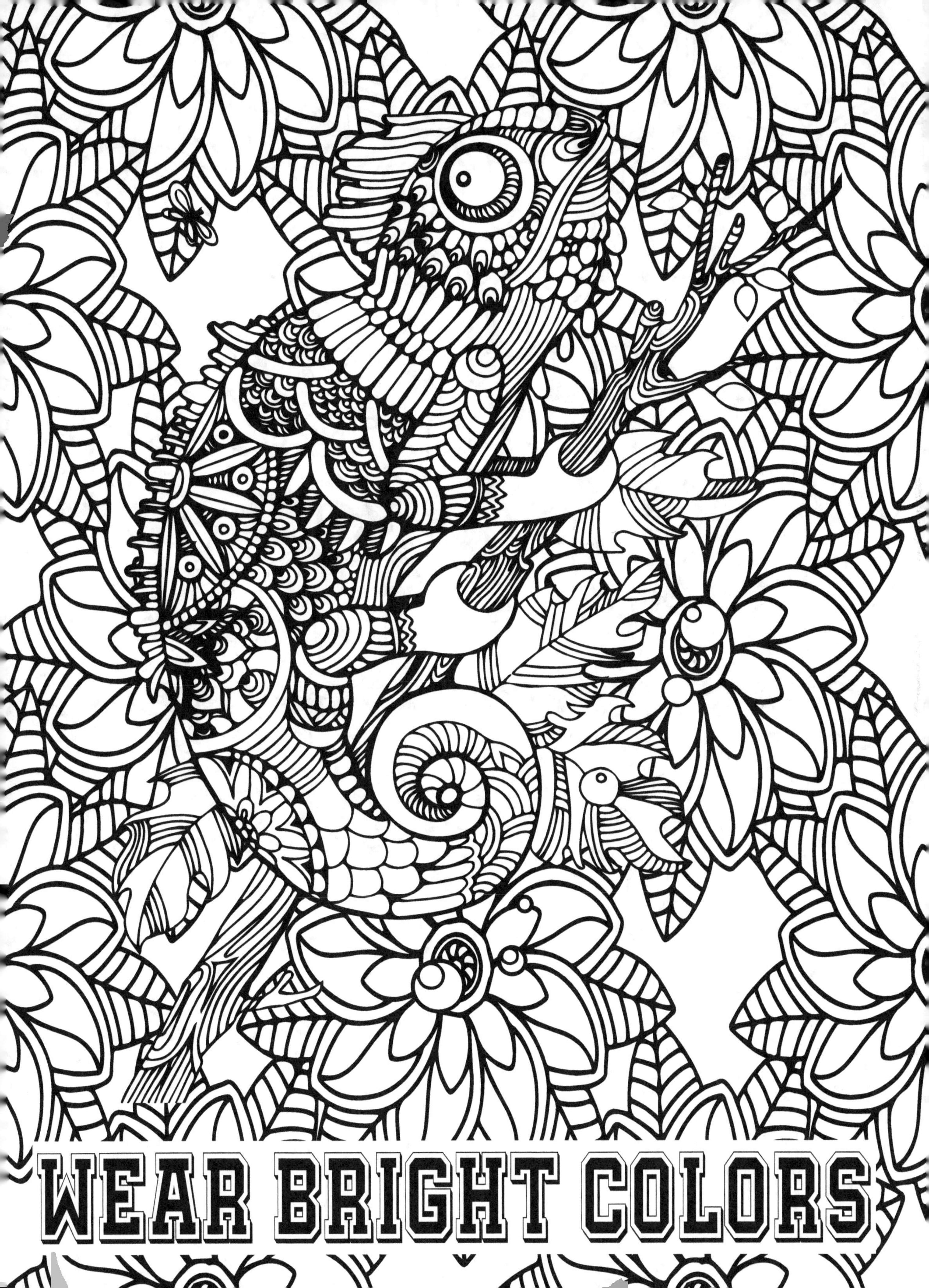
WEAR BRIGHT COLORS

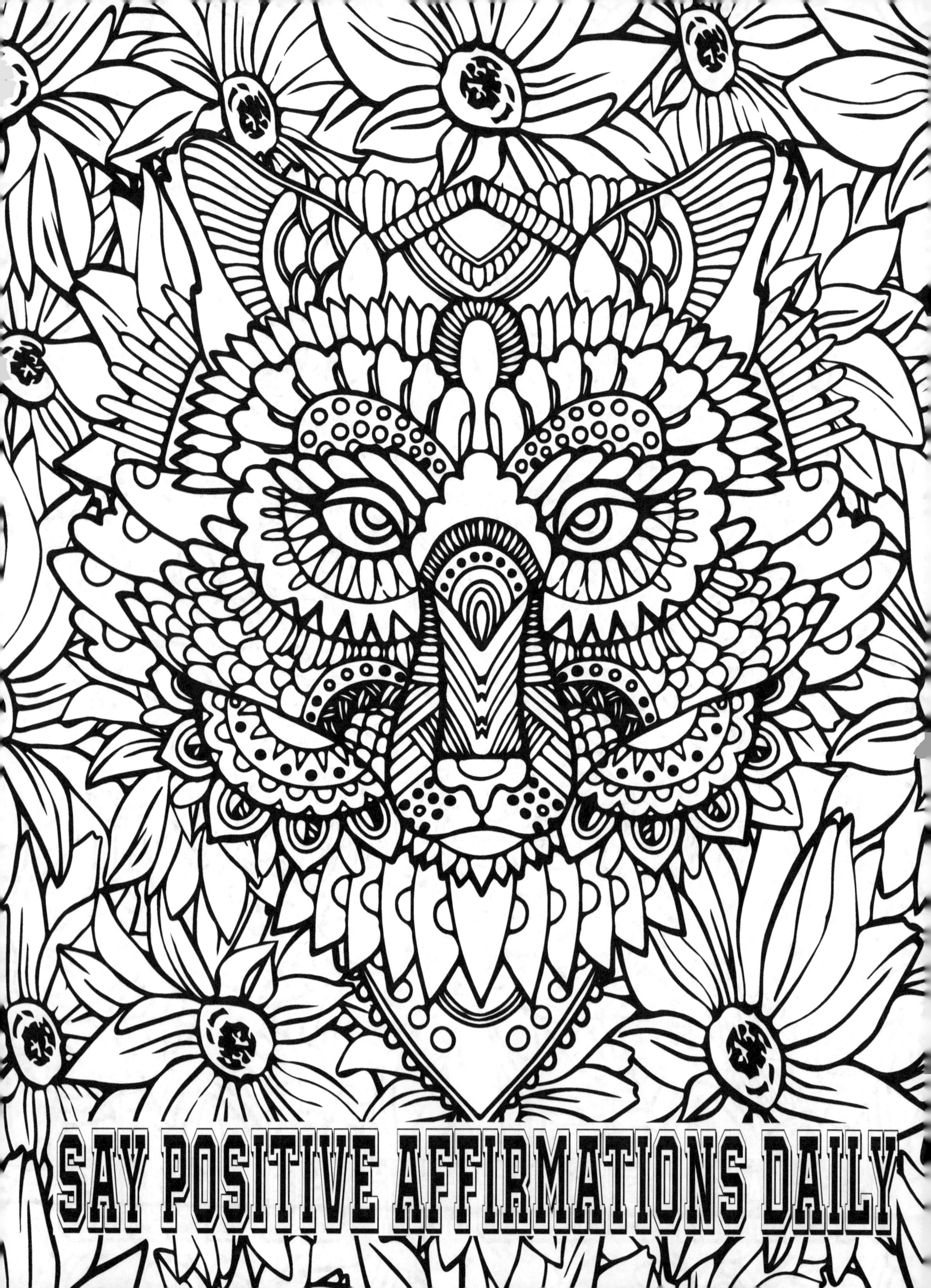
SAY POSITIVE AFFIRMATIONS DAILY

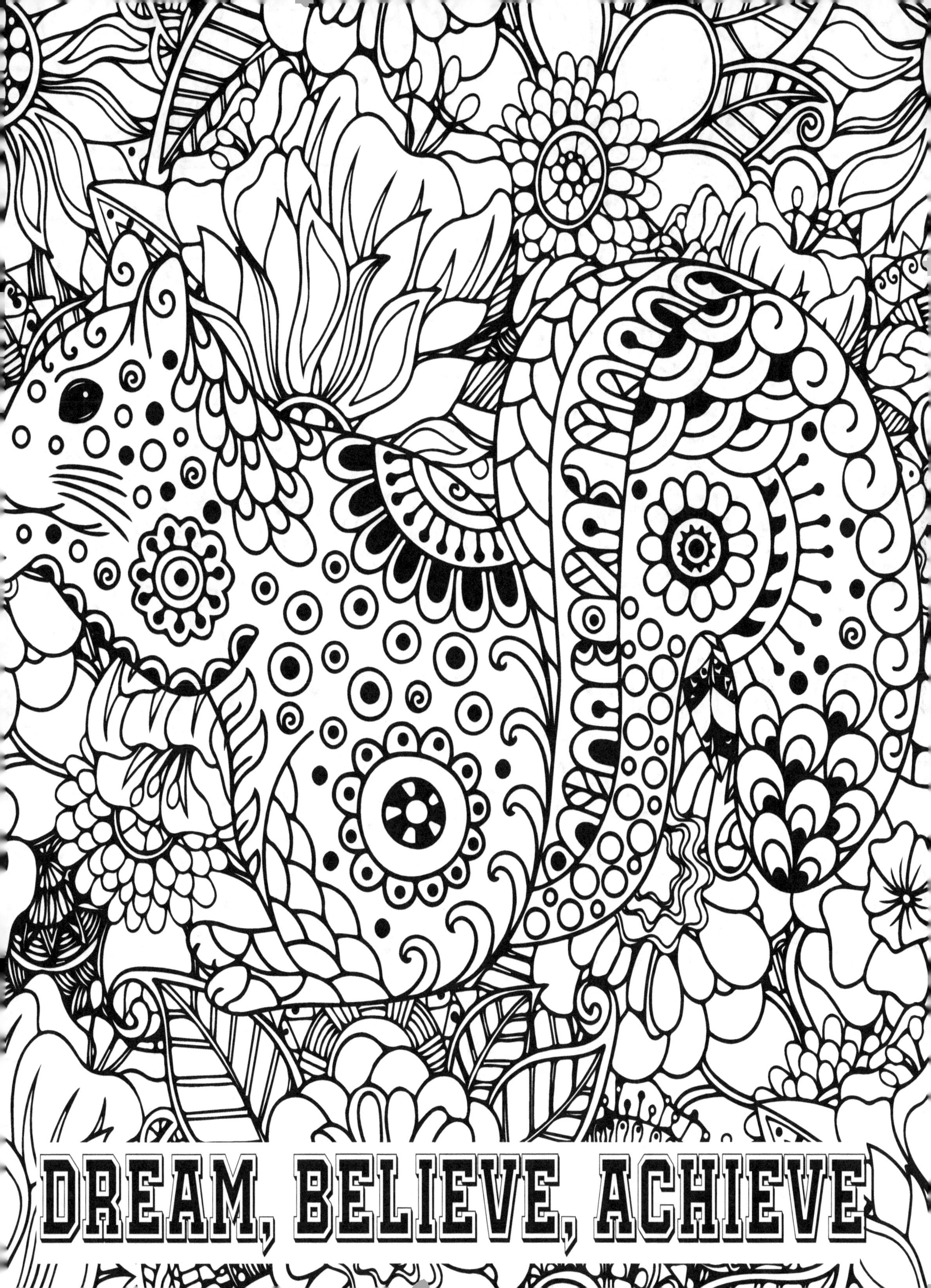
DREAM, BELIEVE, ACHIEVE

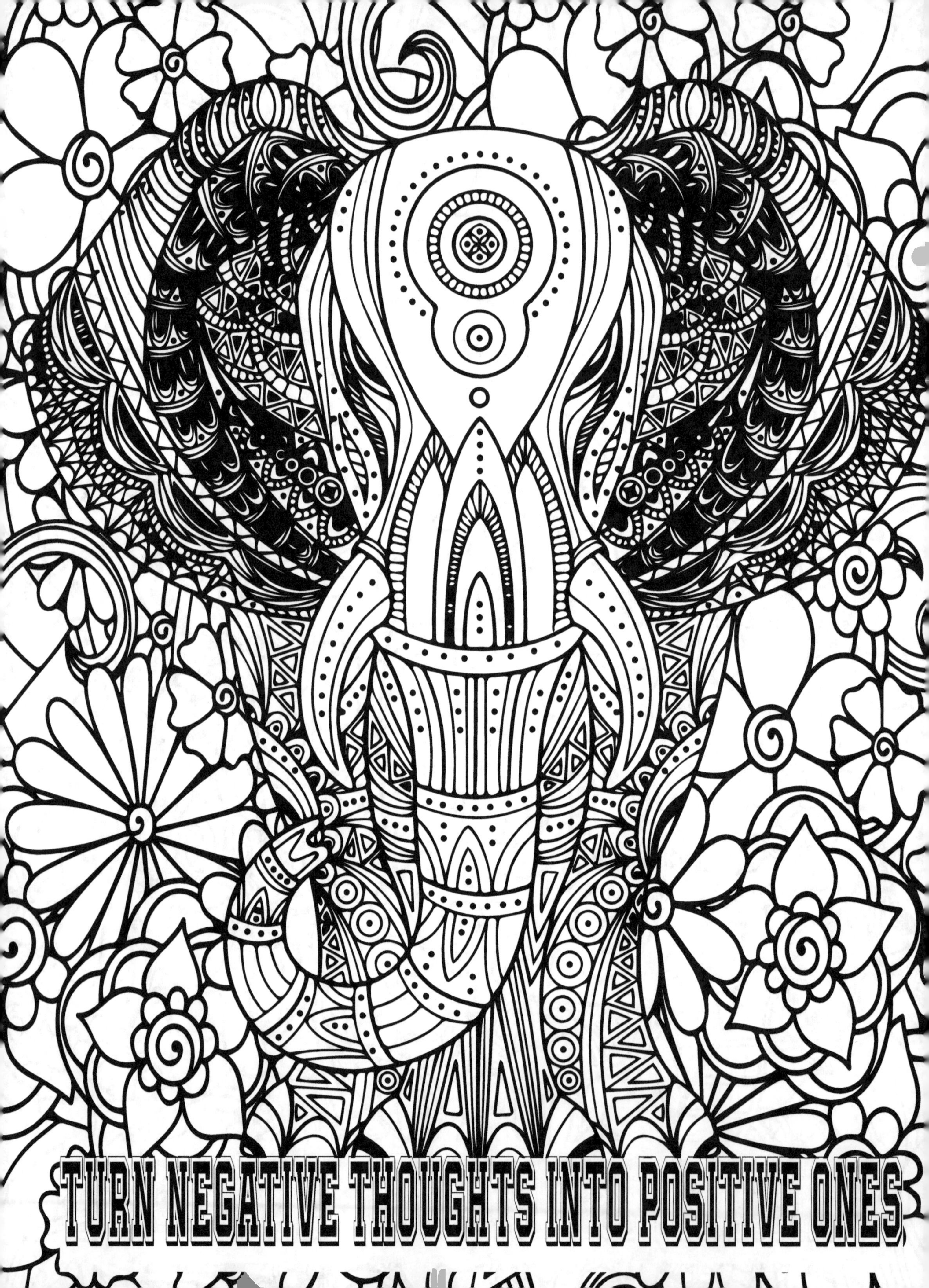
TURN NEGATIVE THOUGHTS INTO POSITIVE ONES

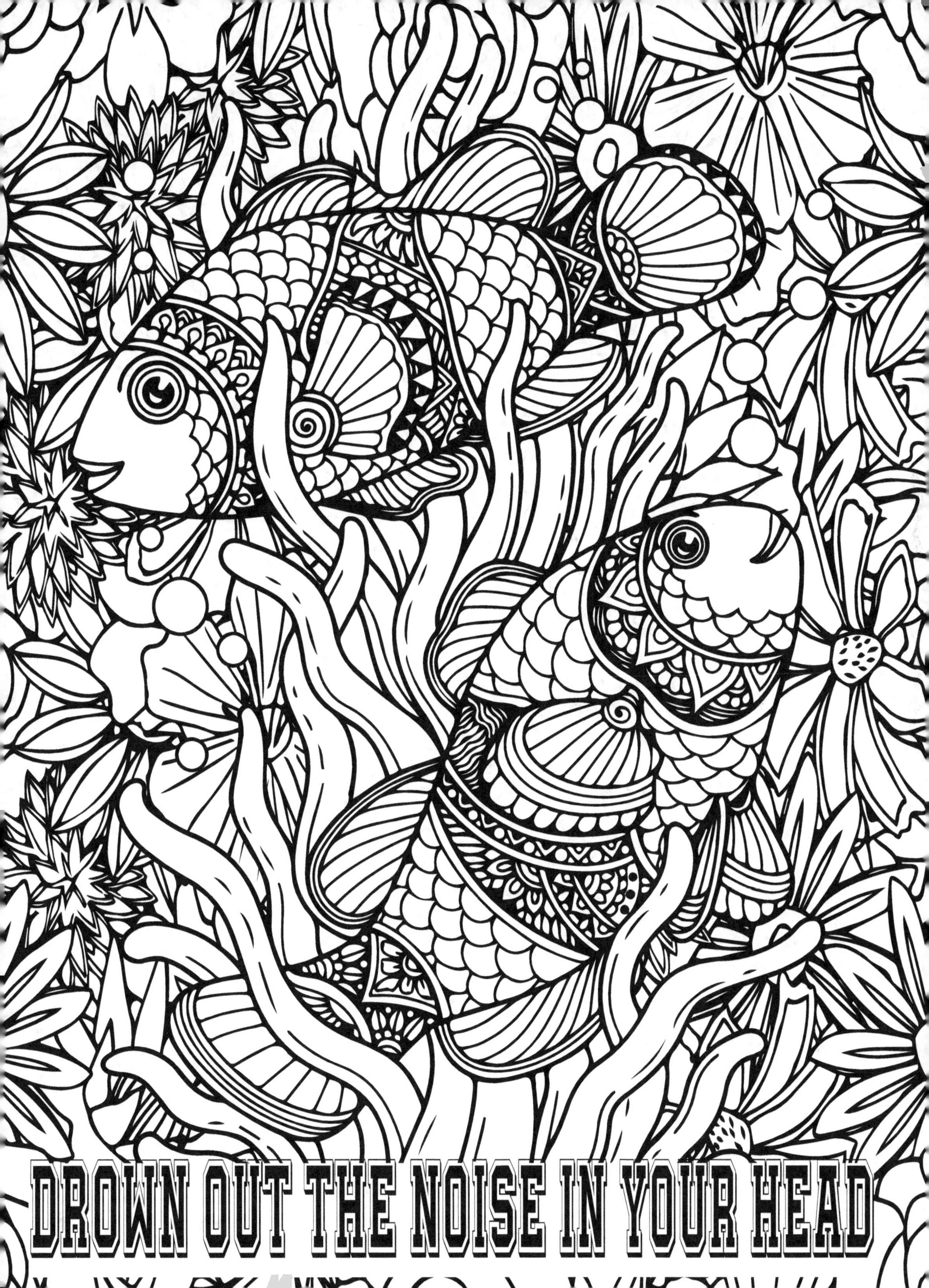
DROWN OUT THE NOISE IN YOUR HEAD

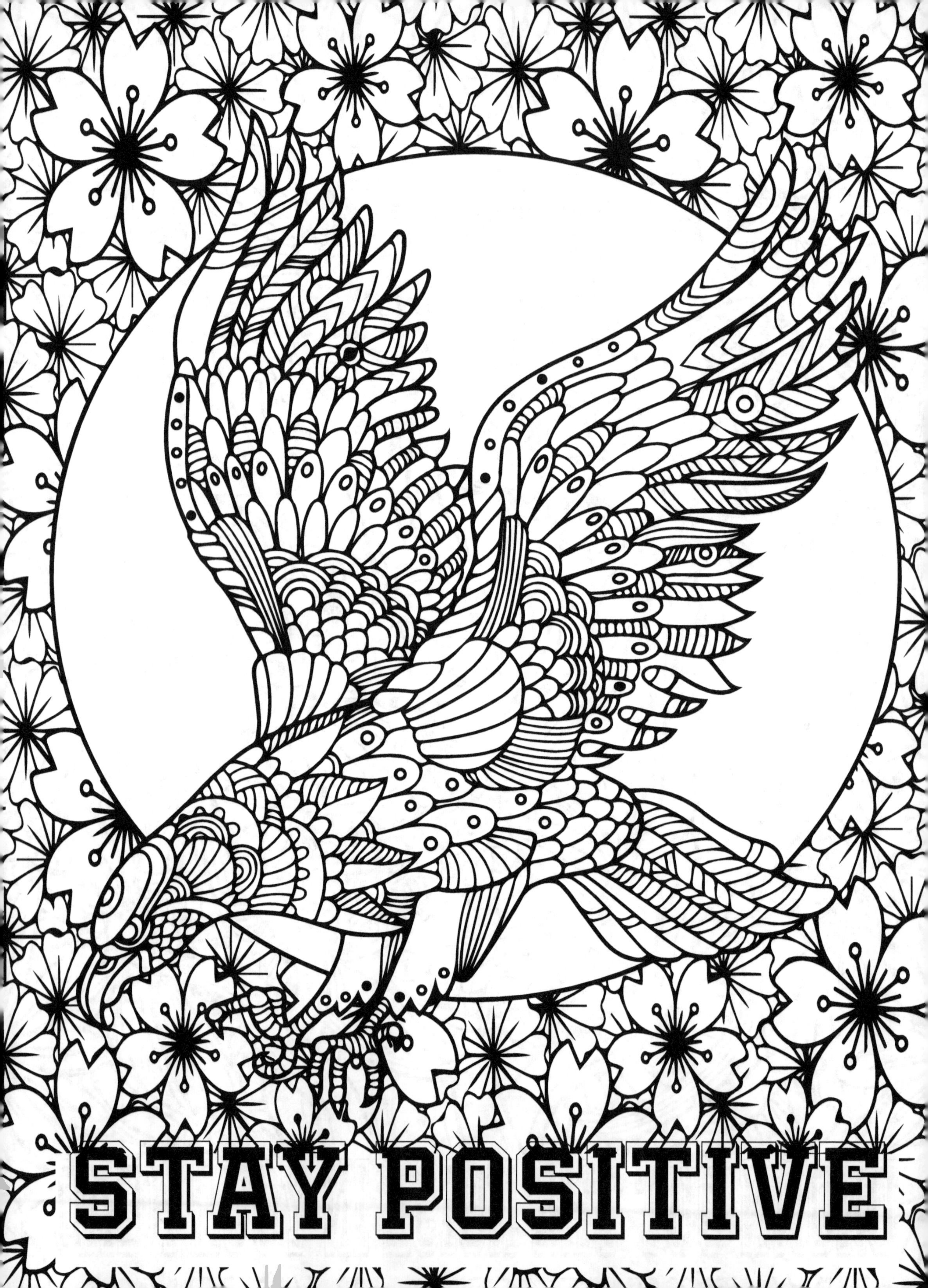
STAY POSITIVE

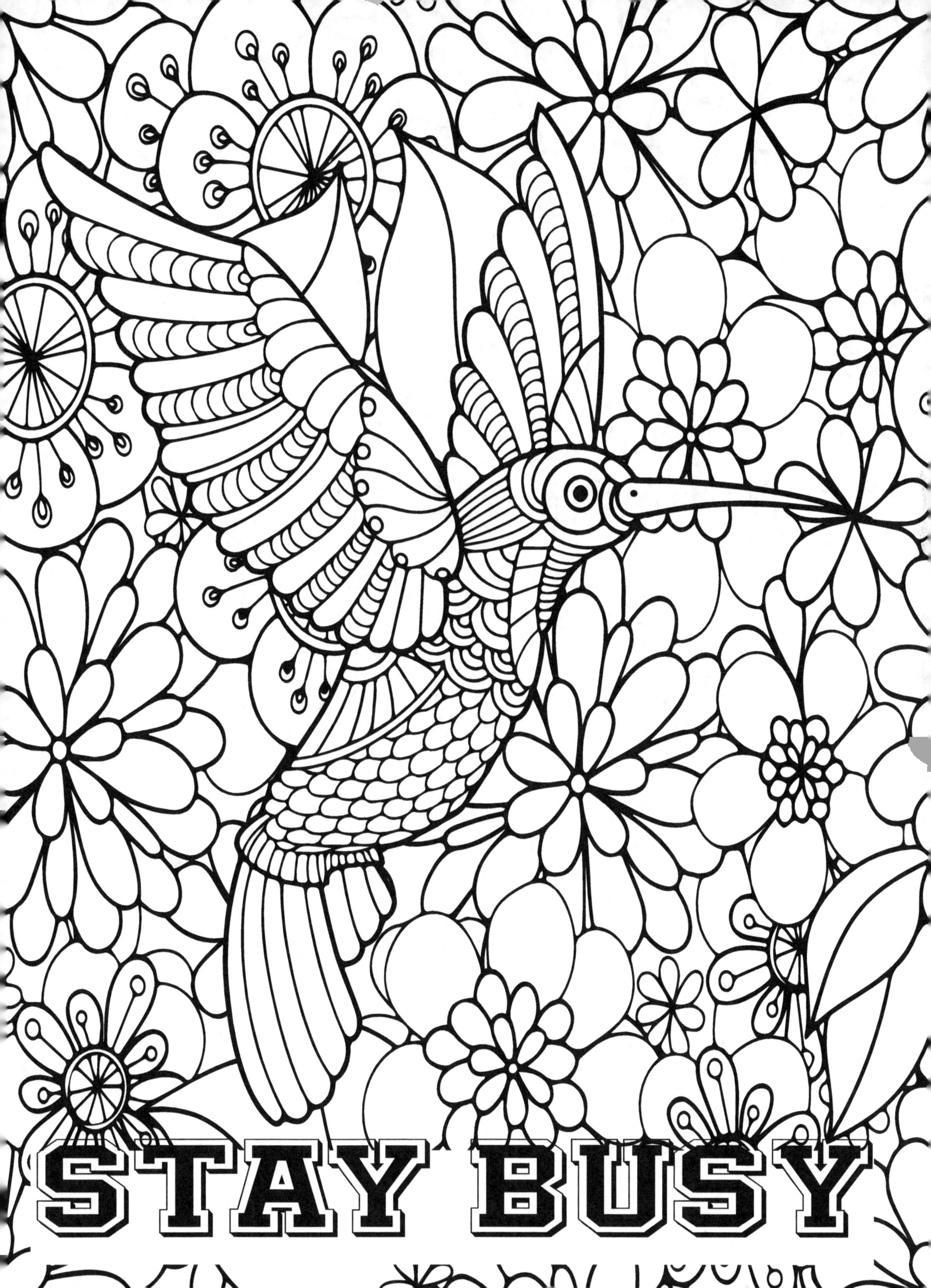
STAY BUSY

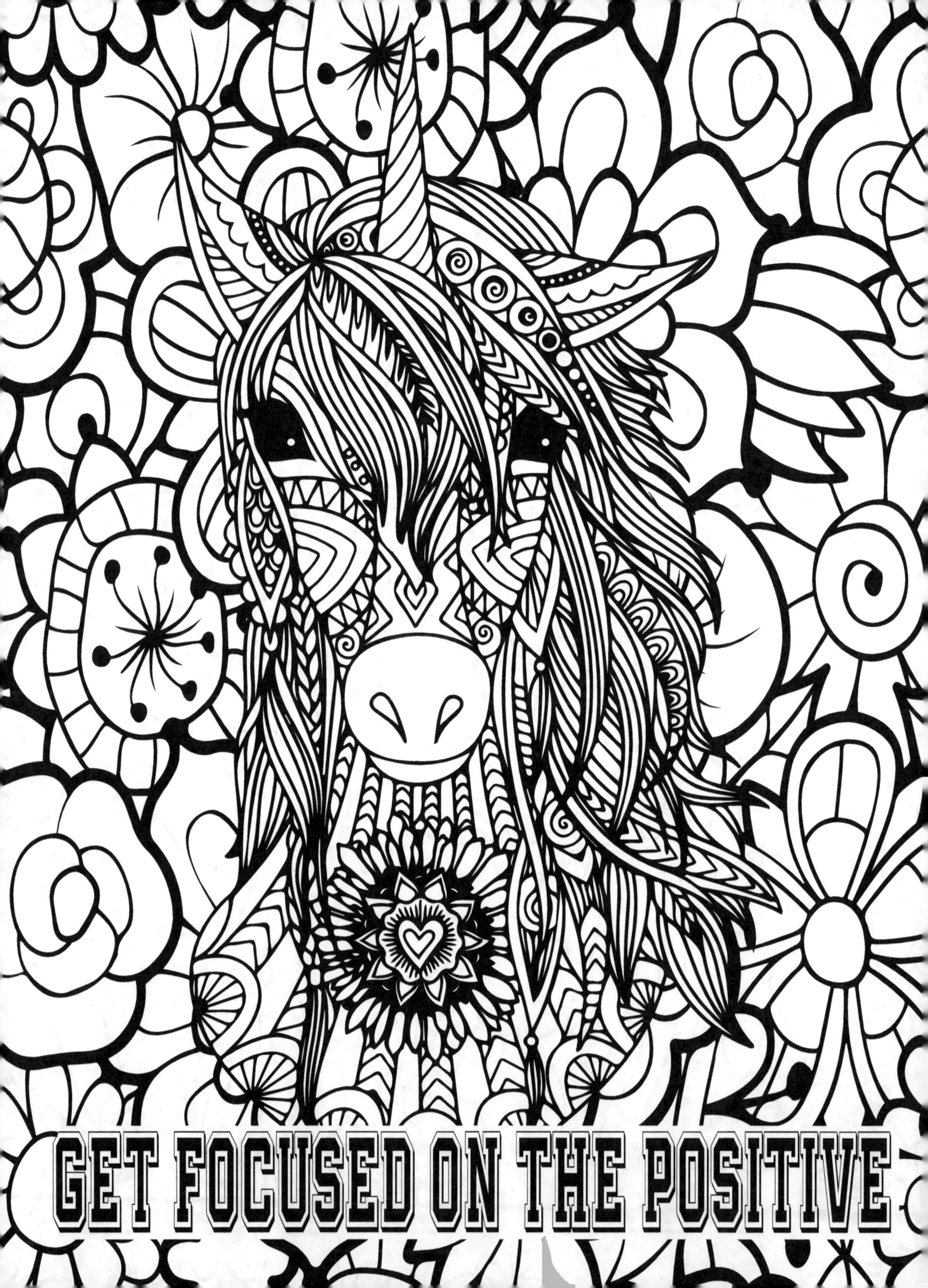
GET FOCUSED ON THE POSITIVE

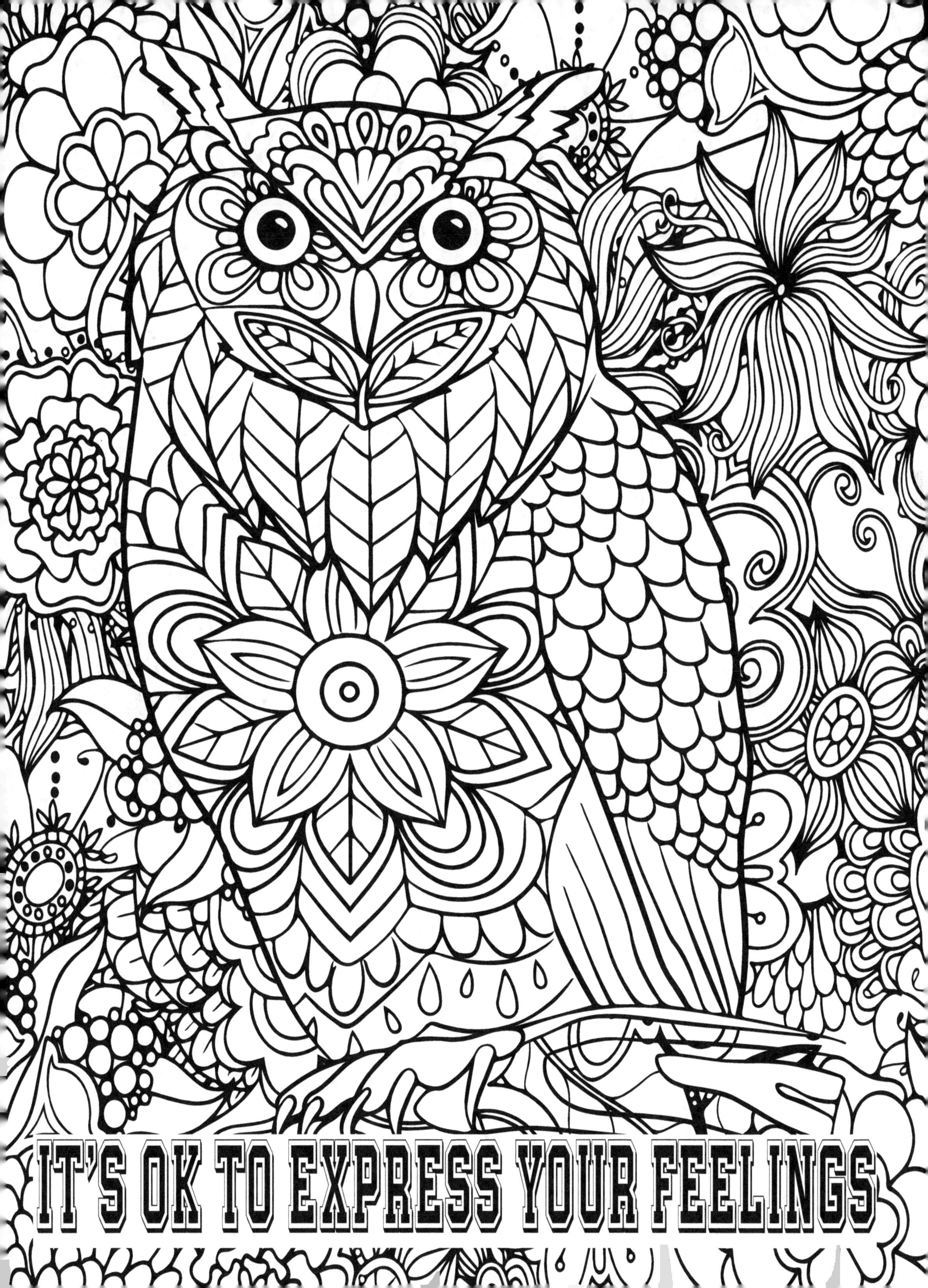
IT'S OK TO EXPRESS YOUR FEELINGS

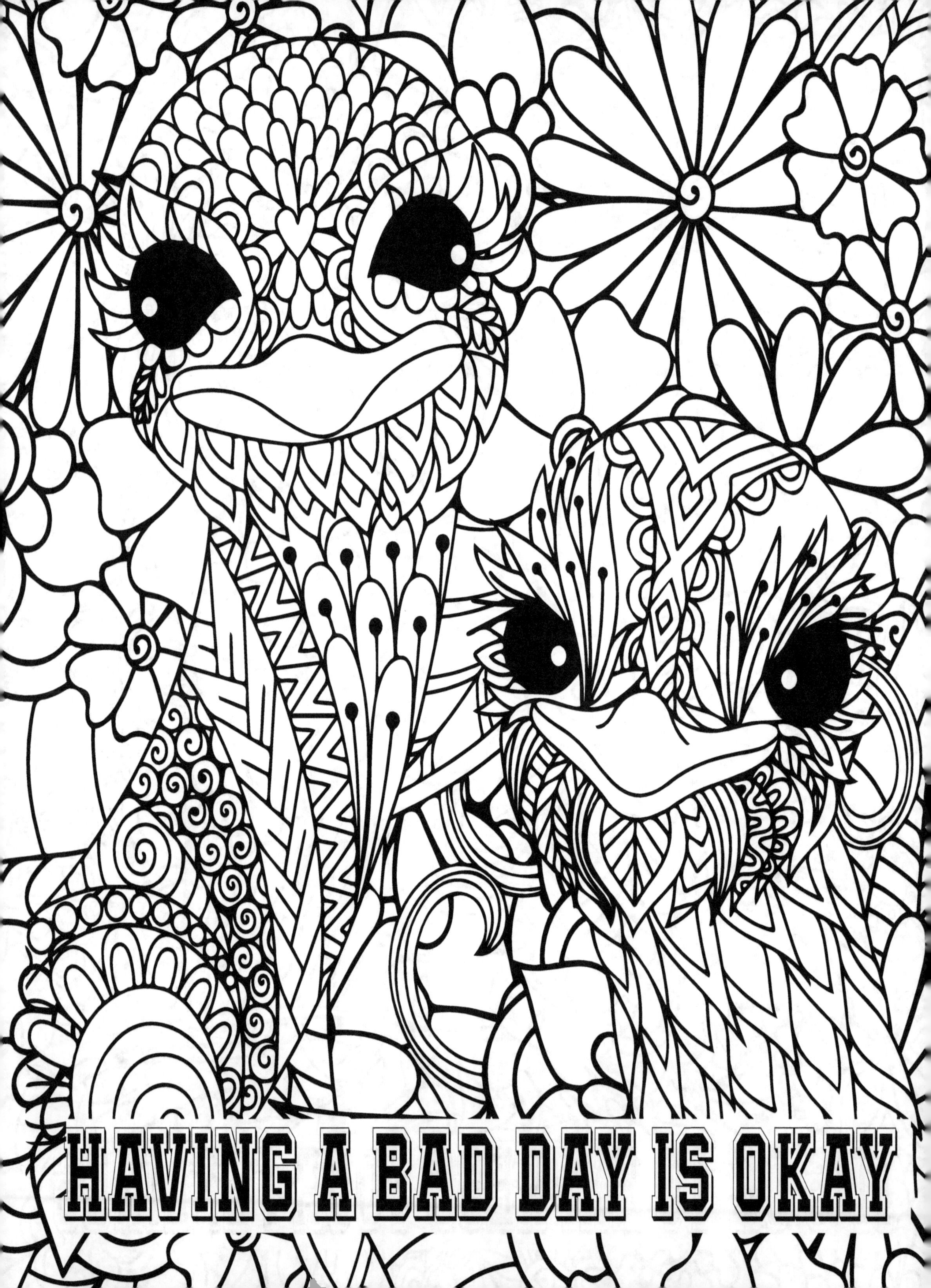
HAVING A BAD DAY IS OKAY

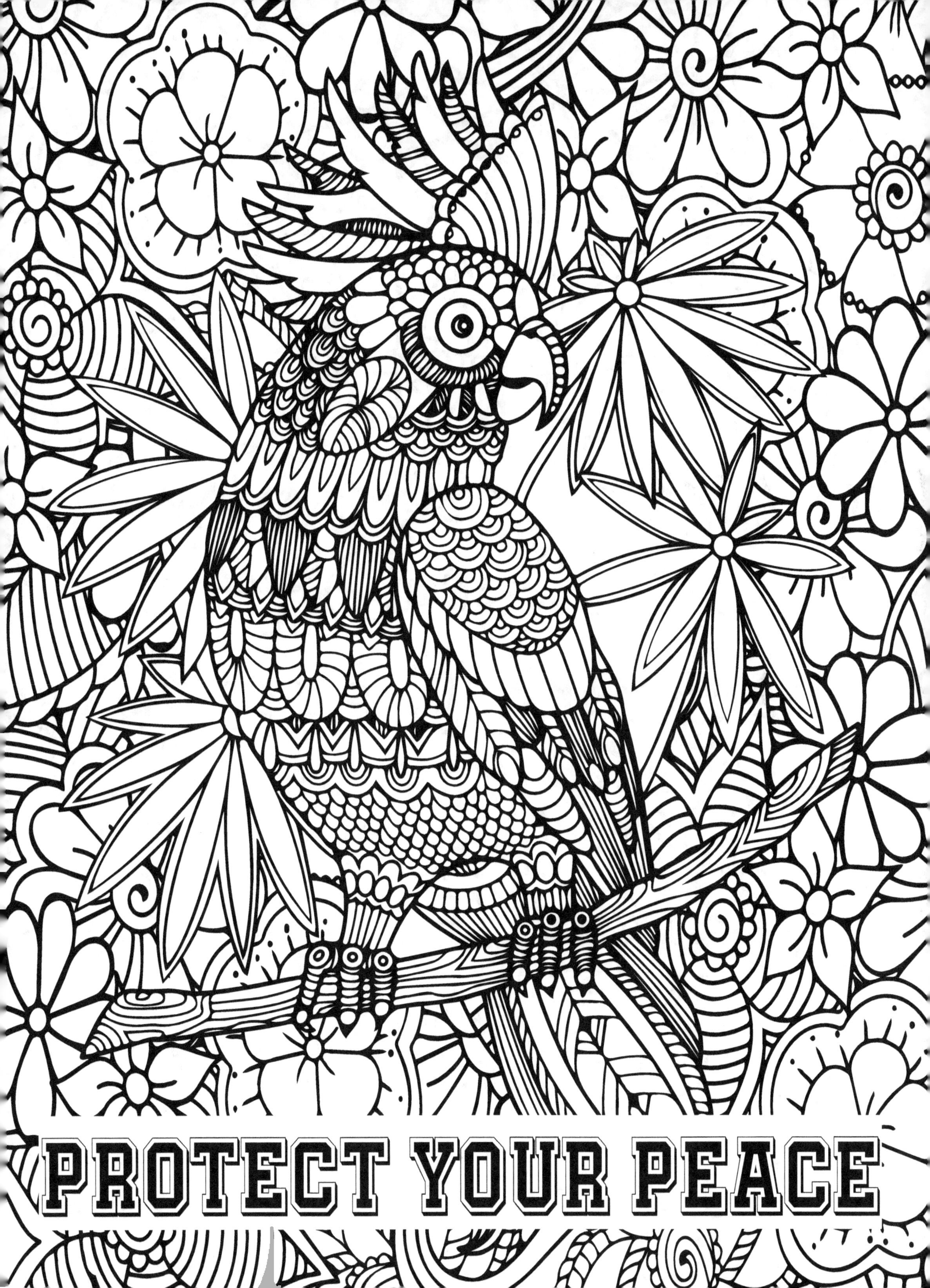
PROTECT YOUR PEACE

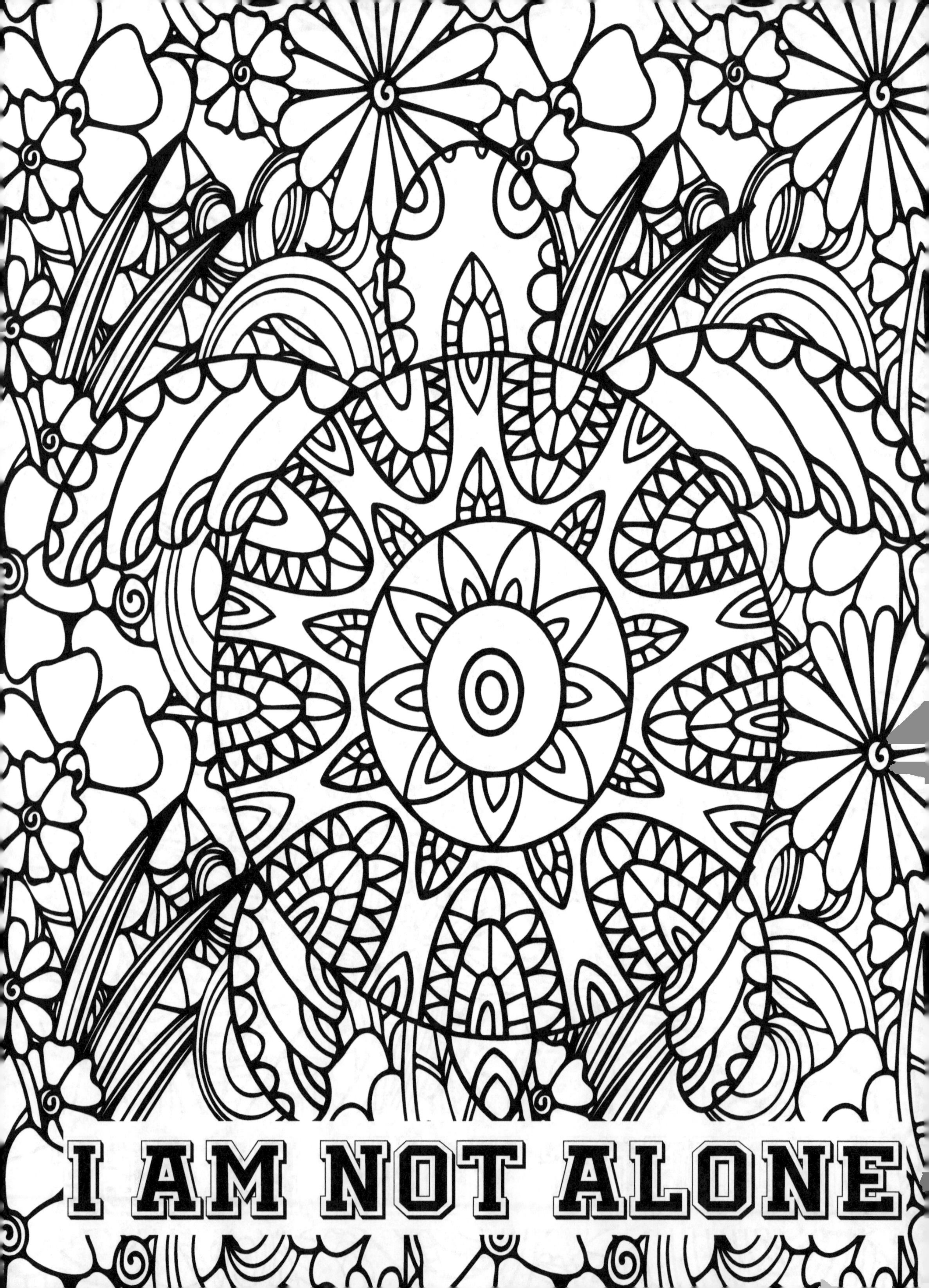
I AM NOT ALONE

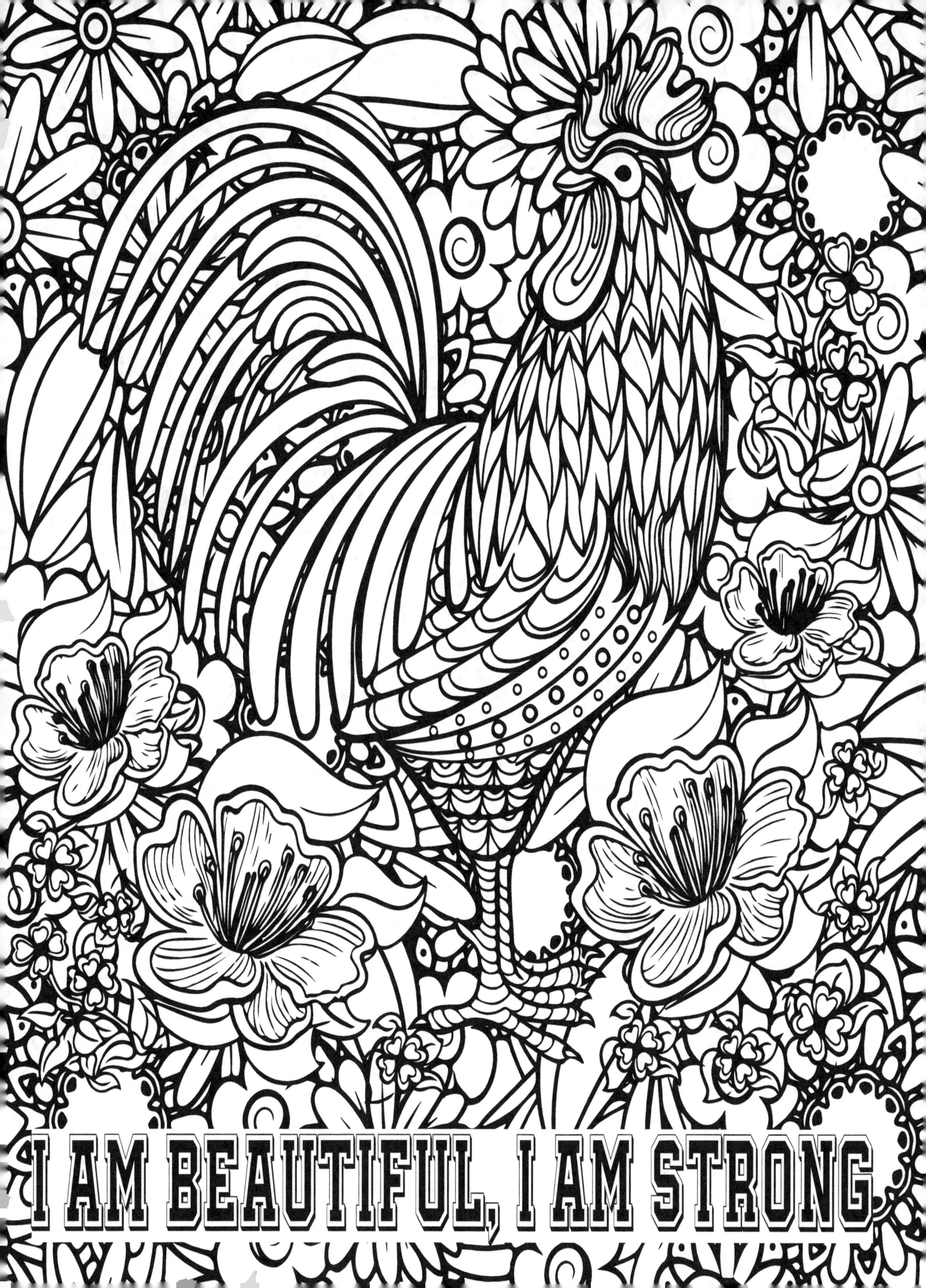
I AM BEAUTIFUL, I AM STRONG.

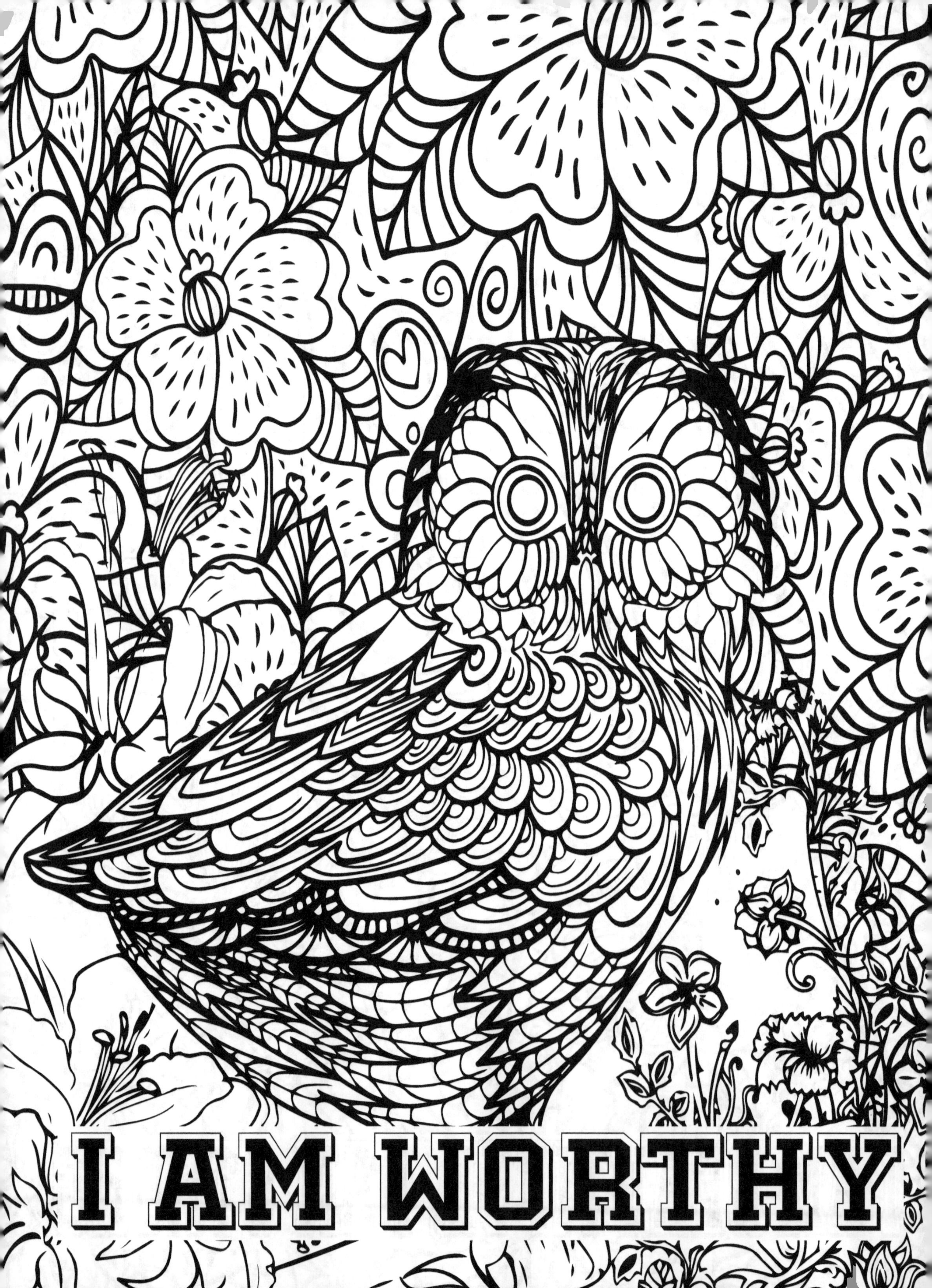
I AM WORTHY

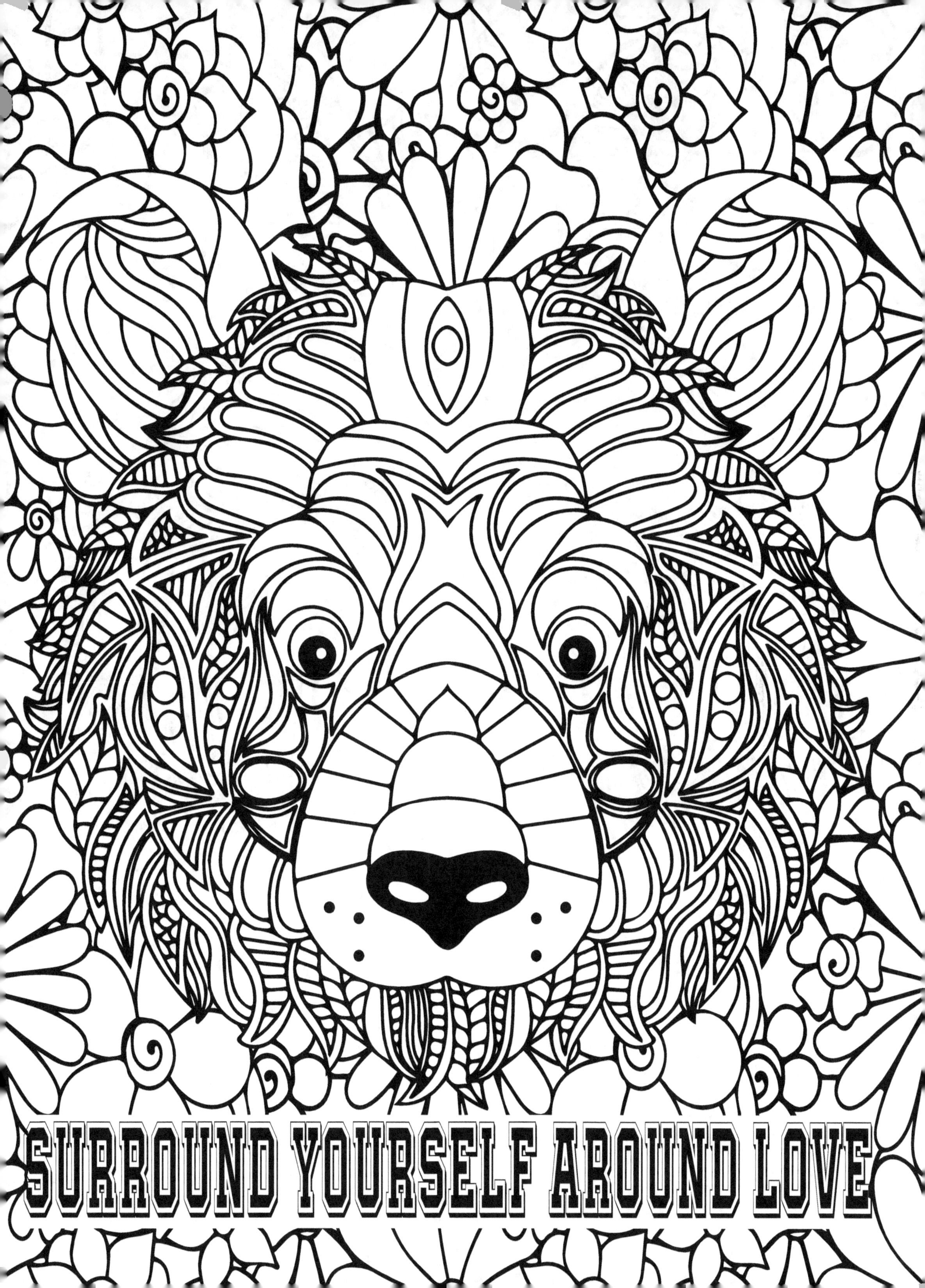
SURROUND YOURSELF AROUND LOVE

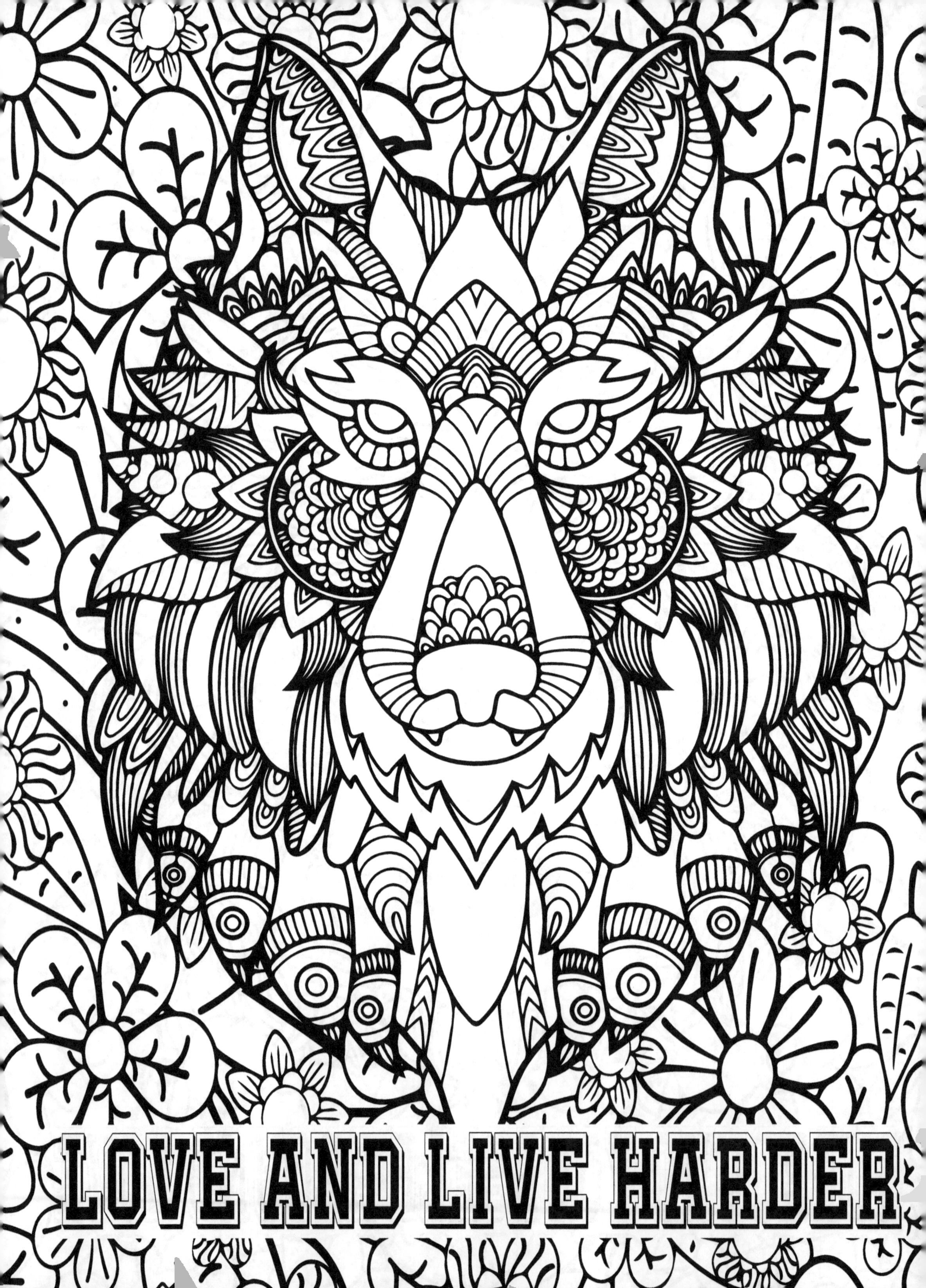
LOVE AND LIVE HARDER

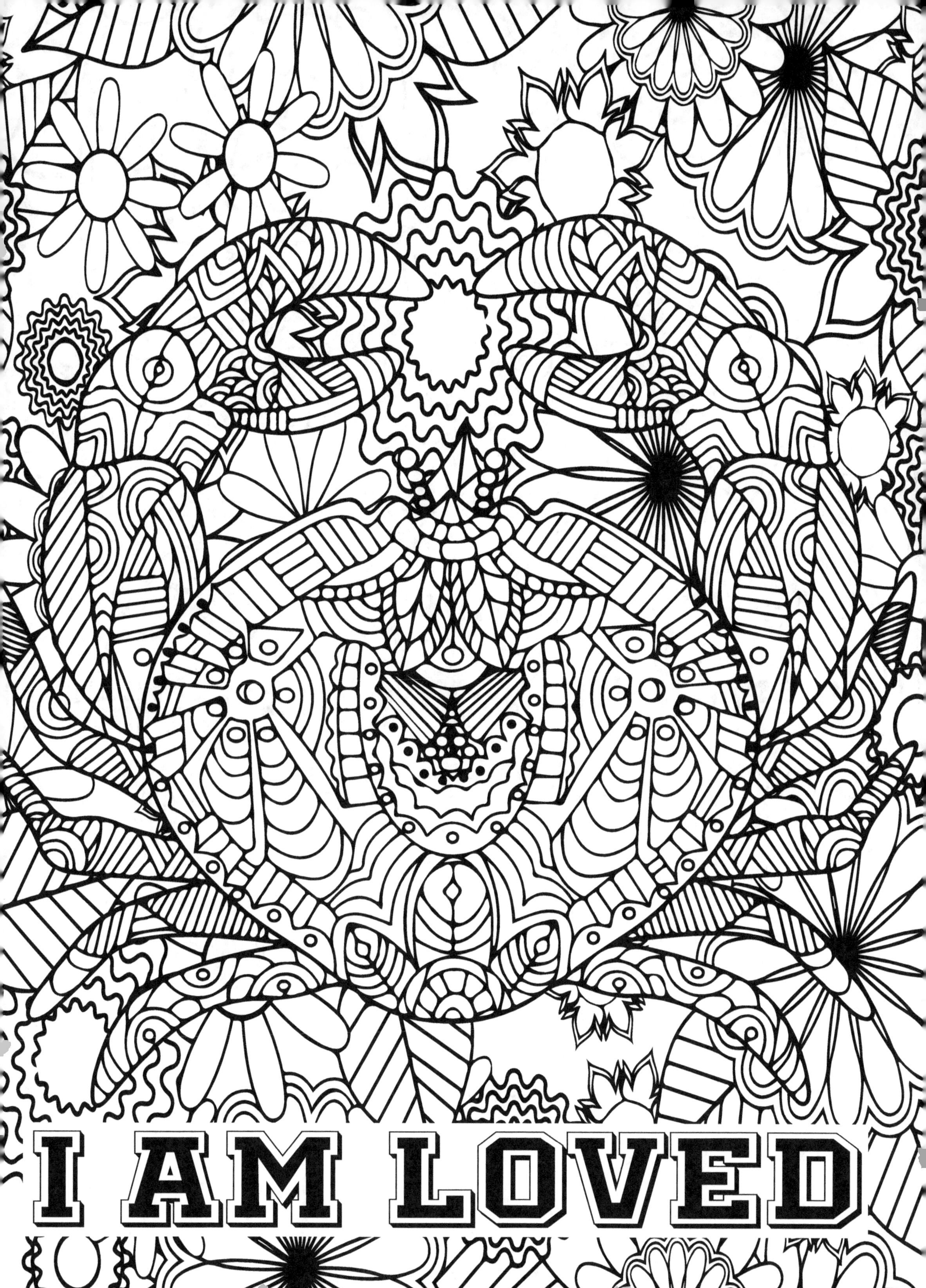
I AM LOVED

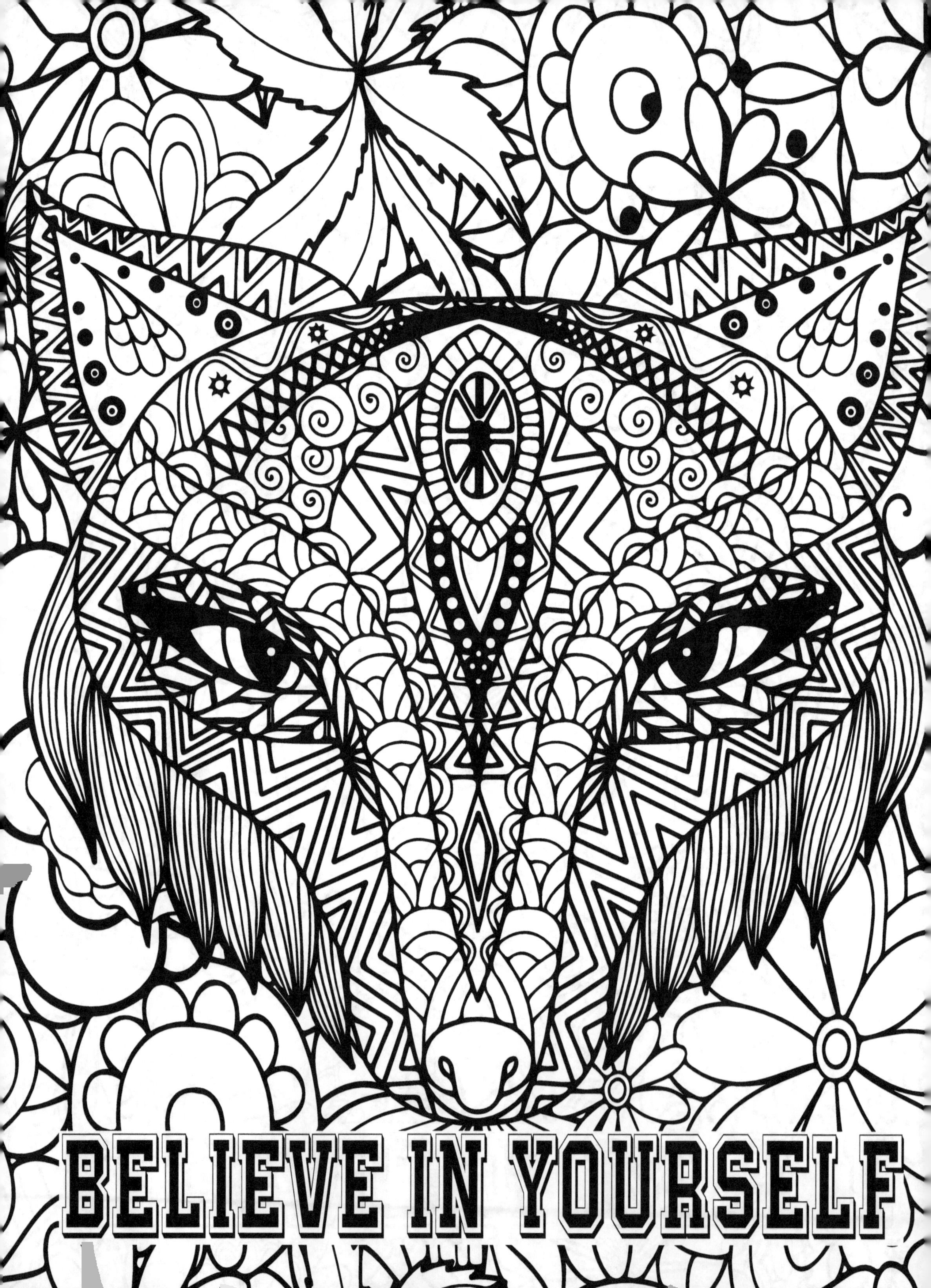
BELIEVE IN YOURSELF

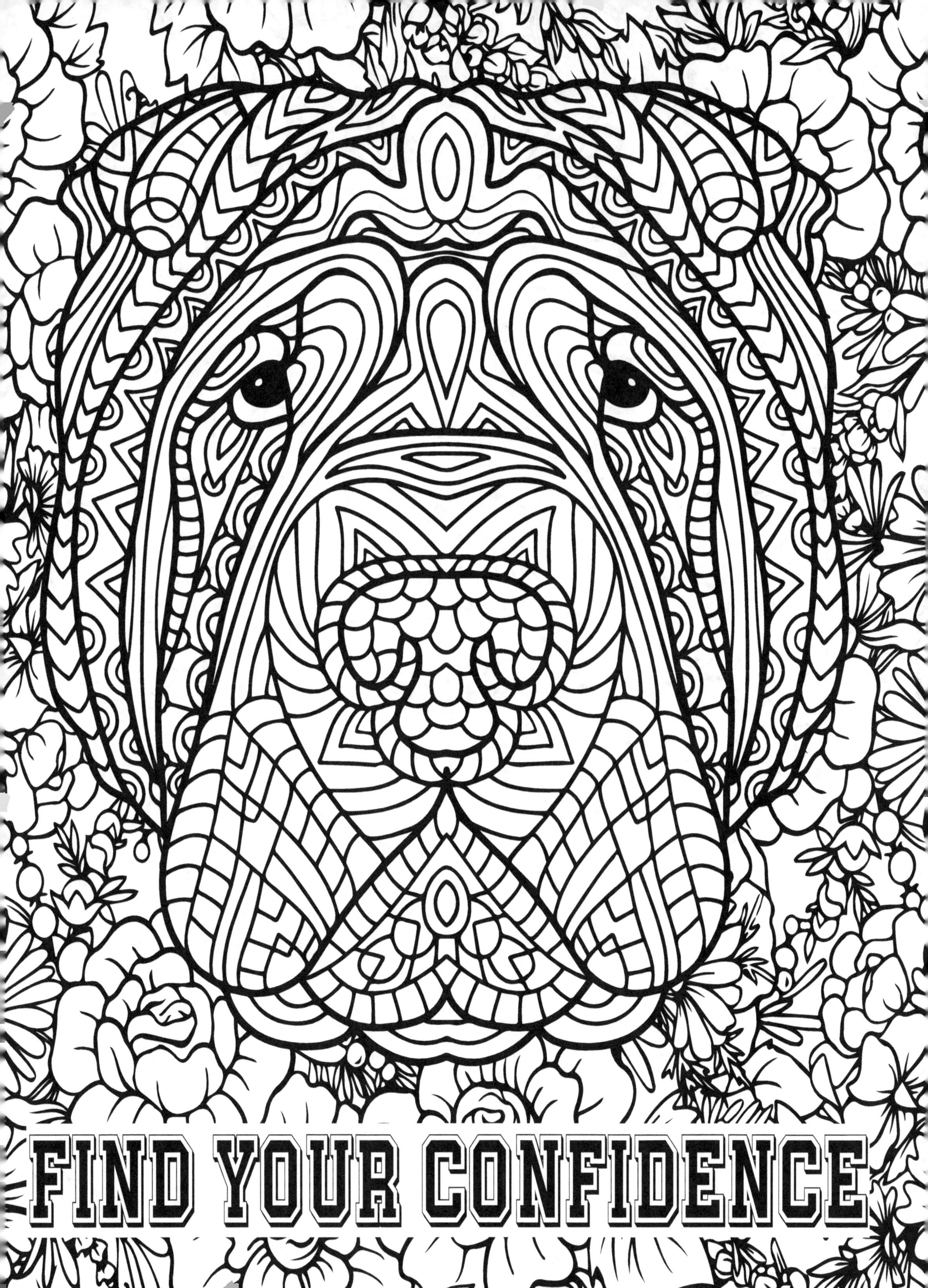
FIND YOUR CONFIDENCE

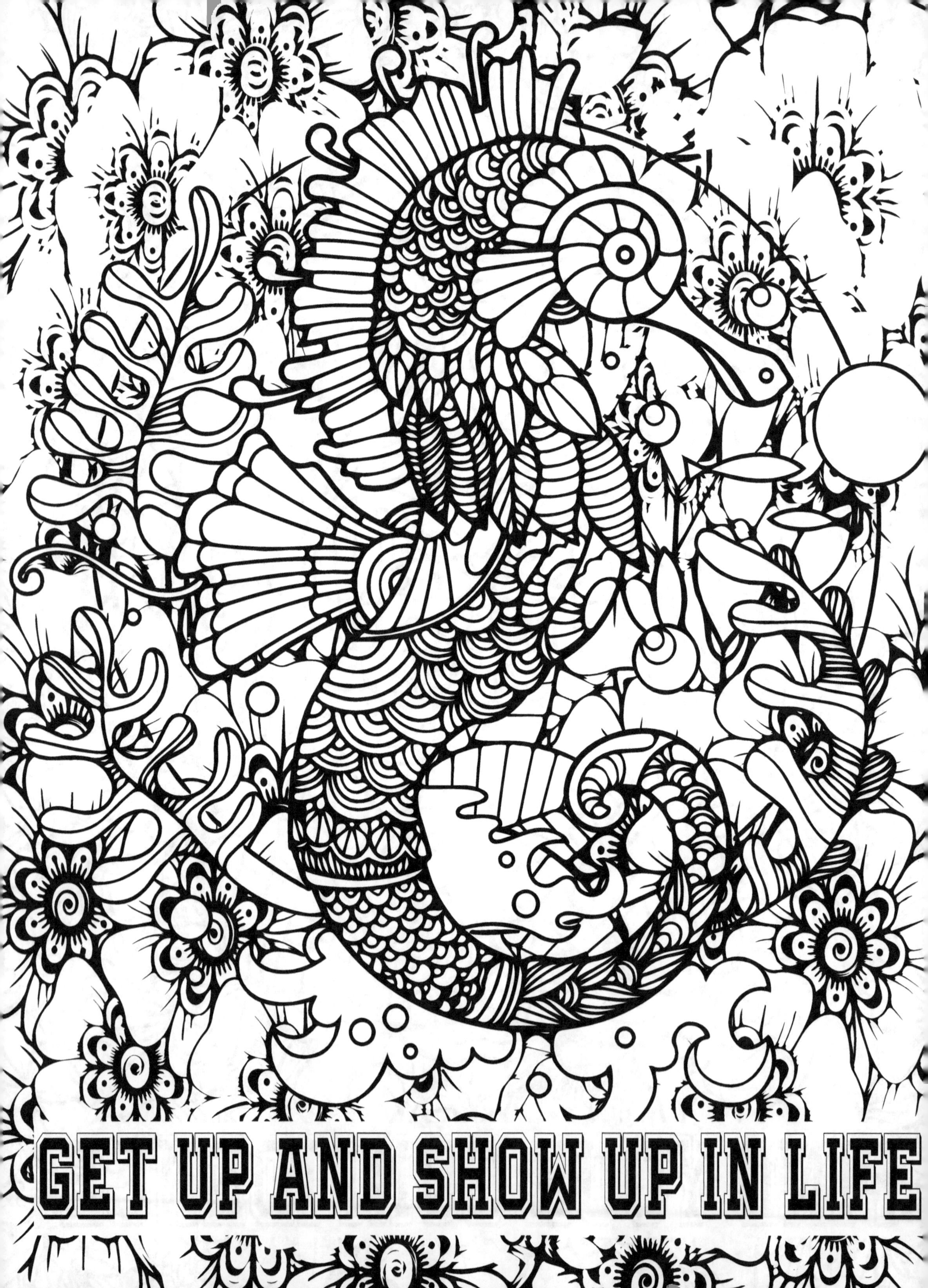
GET UP AND SHOW UP IN LIFE

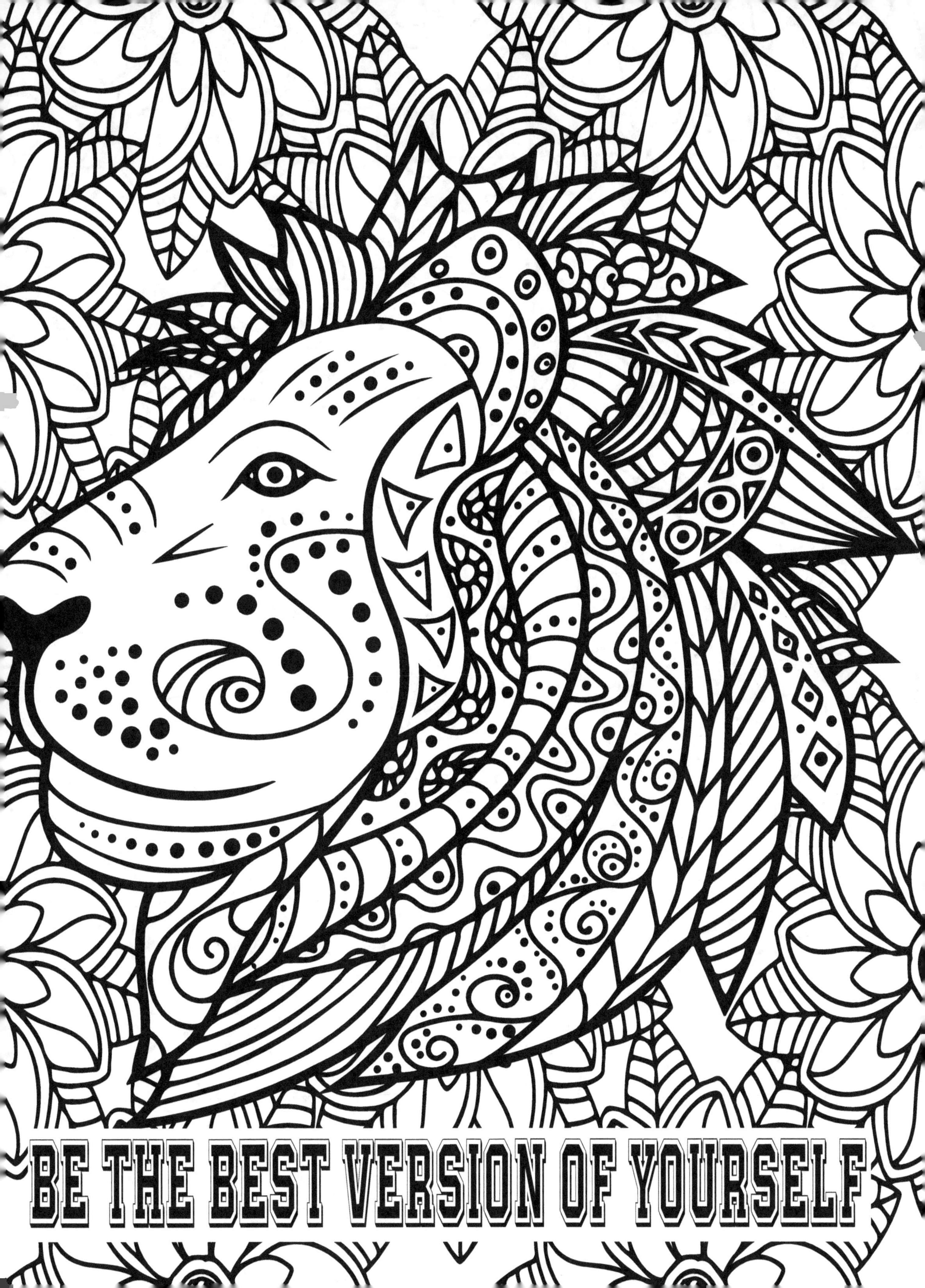
BE THE BEST VERSION OF YOURSELF

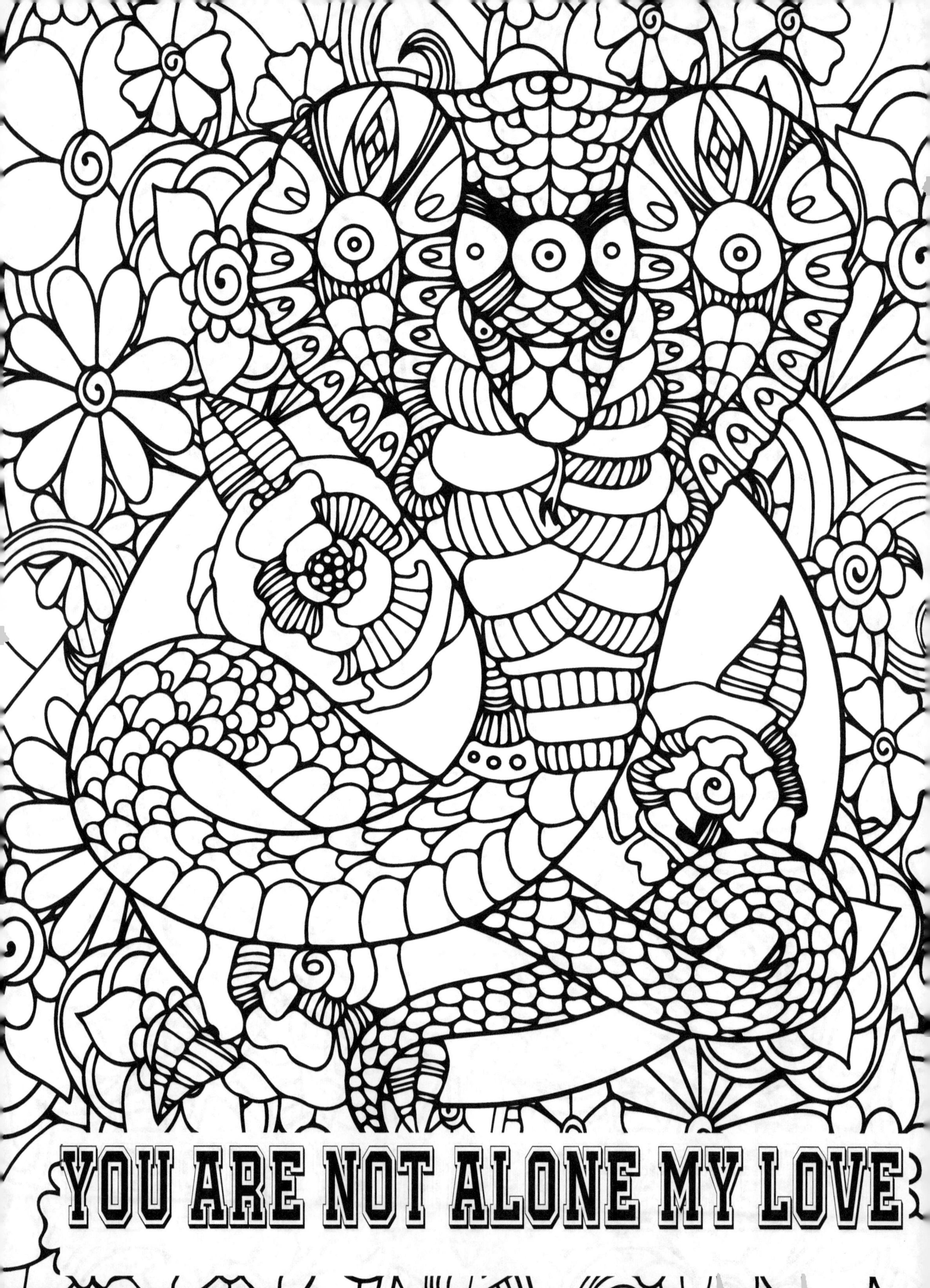
YOU ARE NOT ALONE MY LOVE

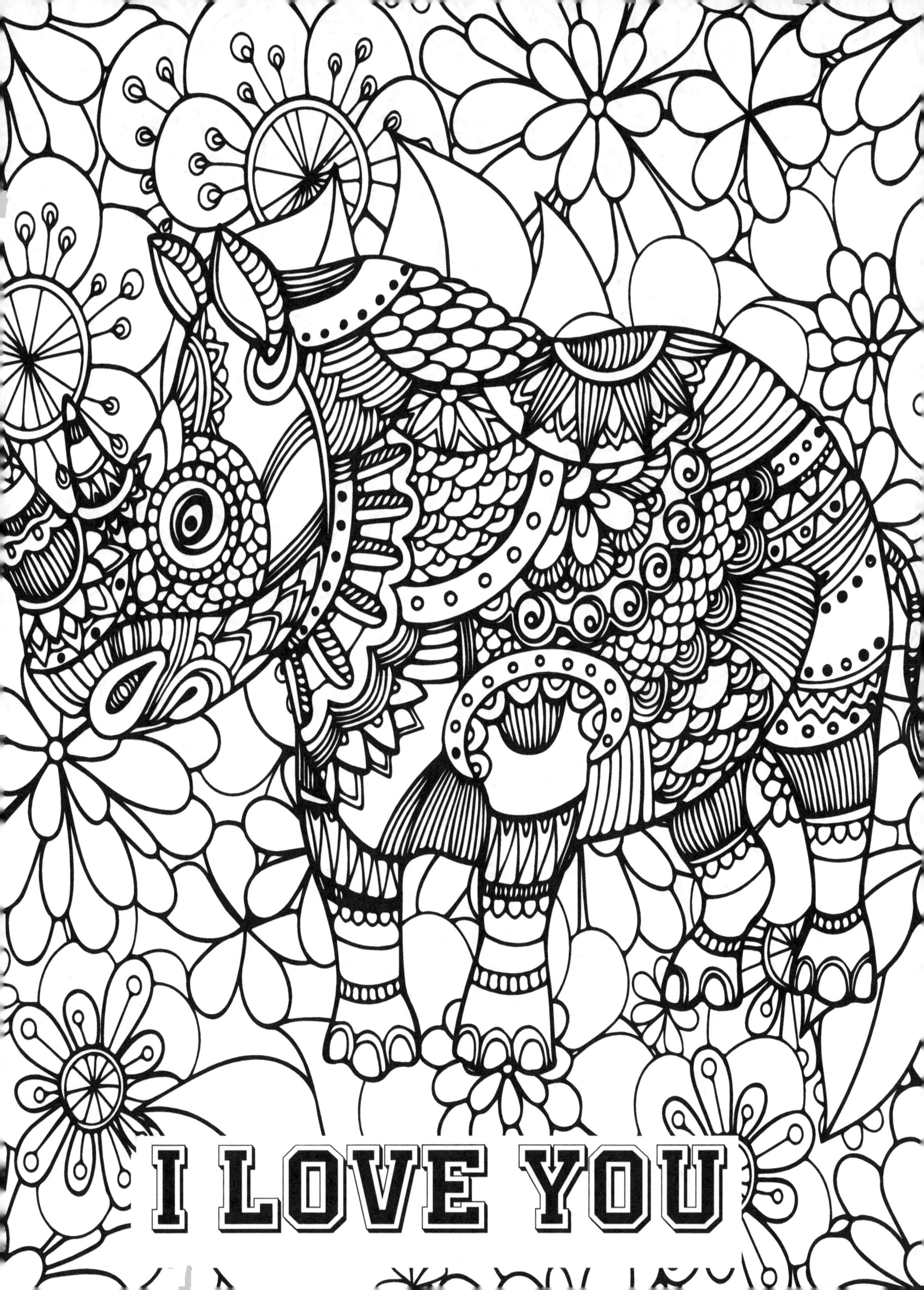
I LOVE YOU

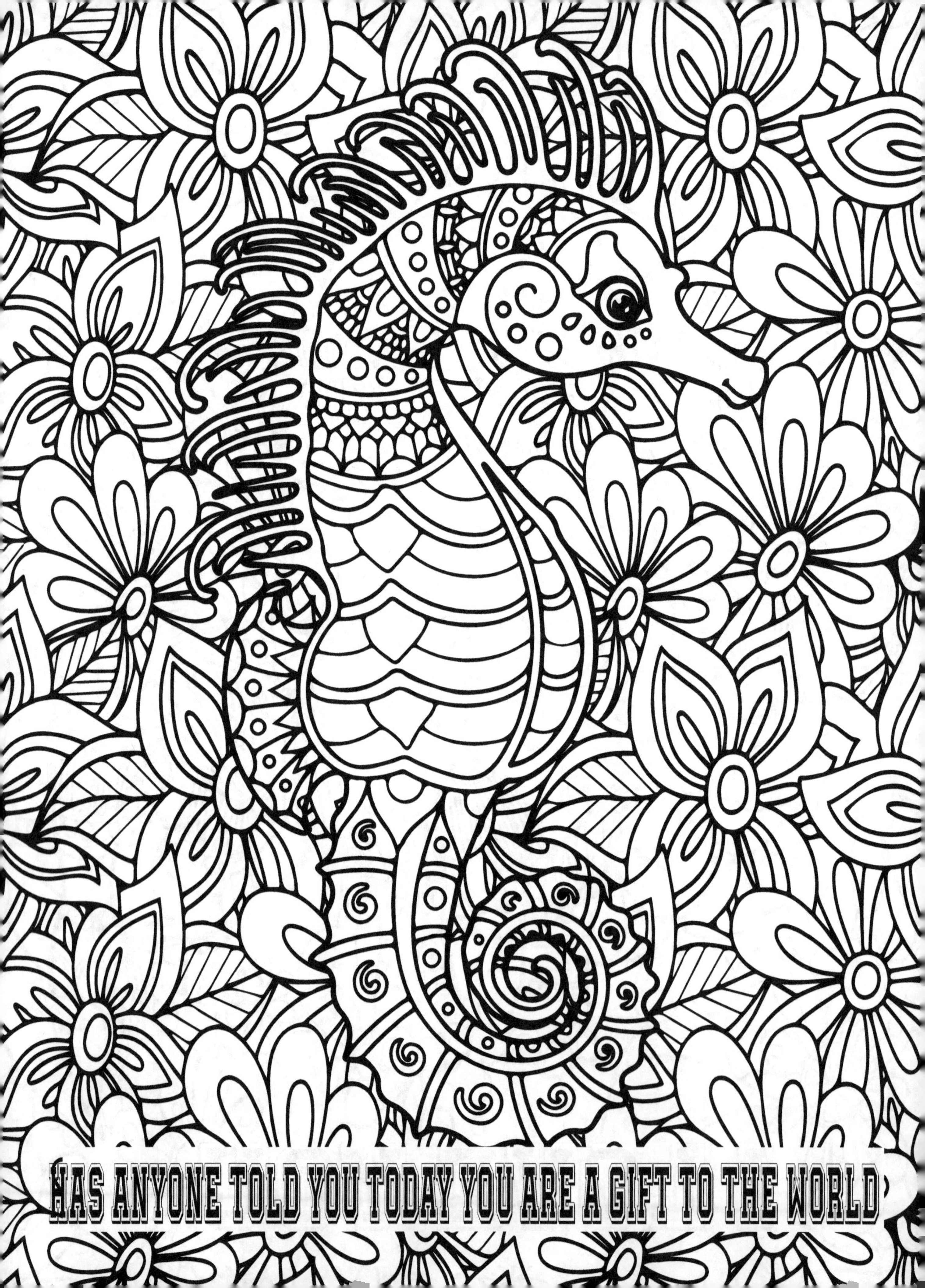
HAS ANYONE TOLD YOU TODAY YOU ARE A GIFT TO THE WORLD

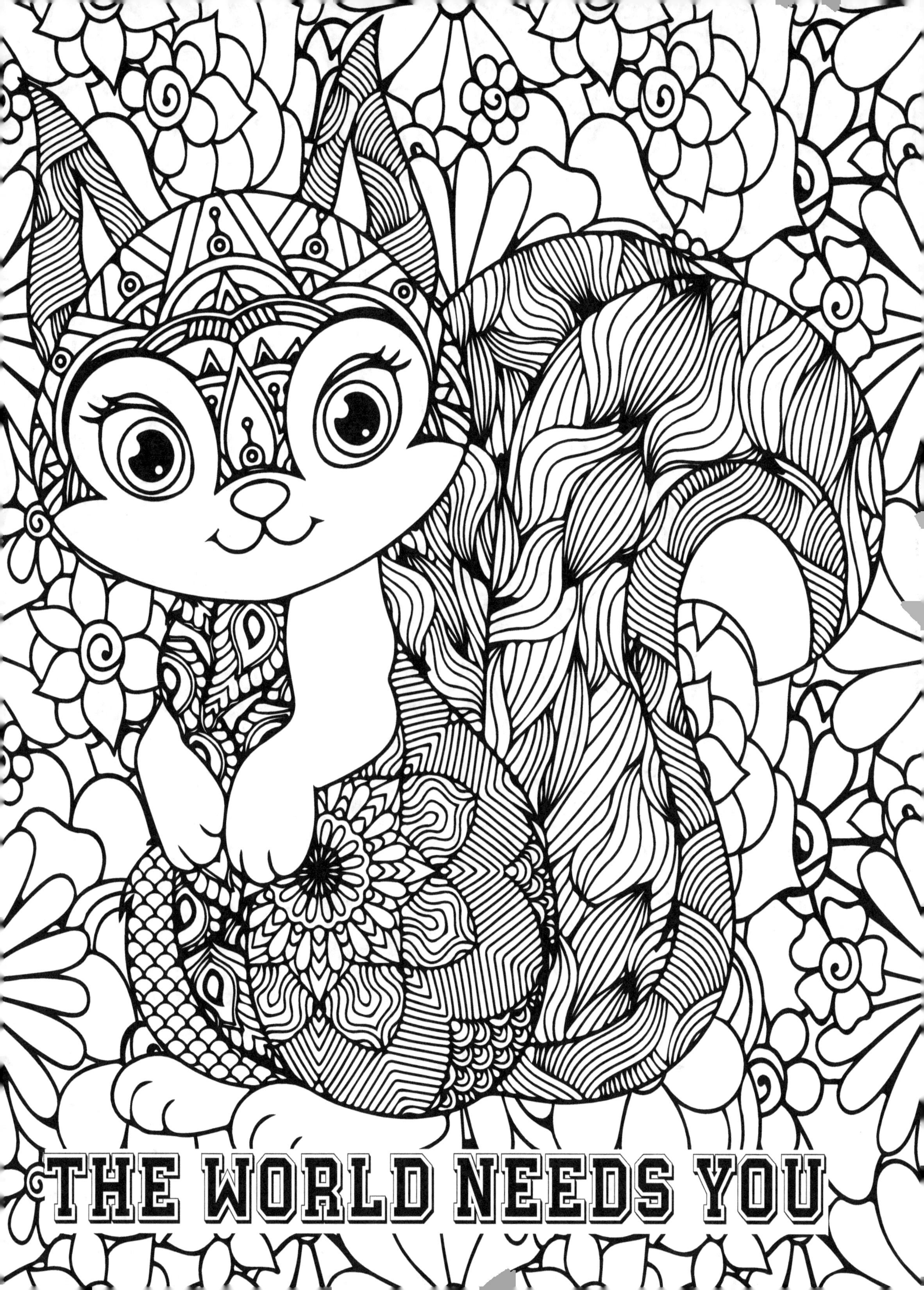
THE WORLD NEEDS YOU

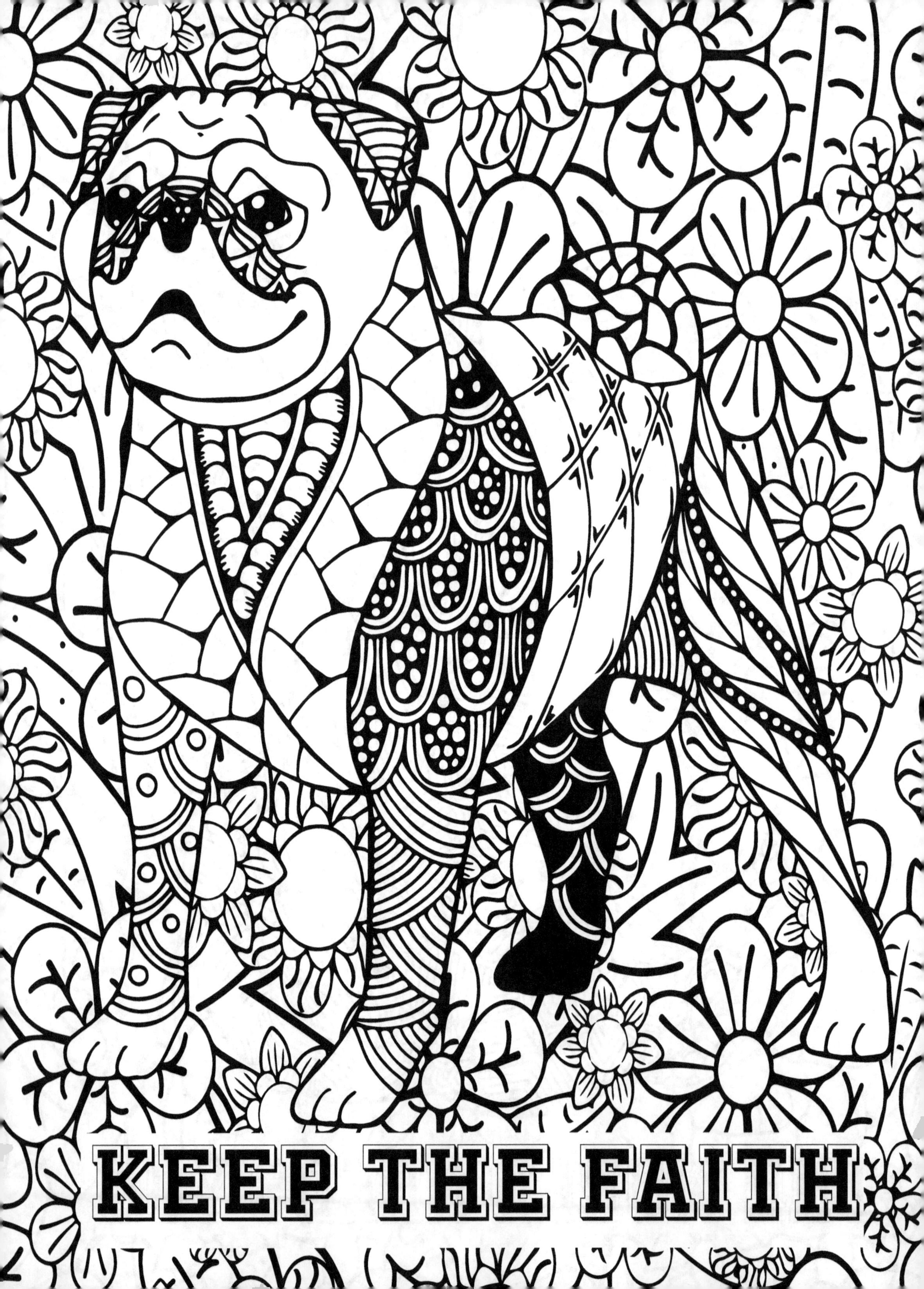
KEEP THE FAITH

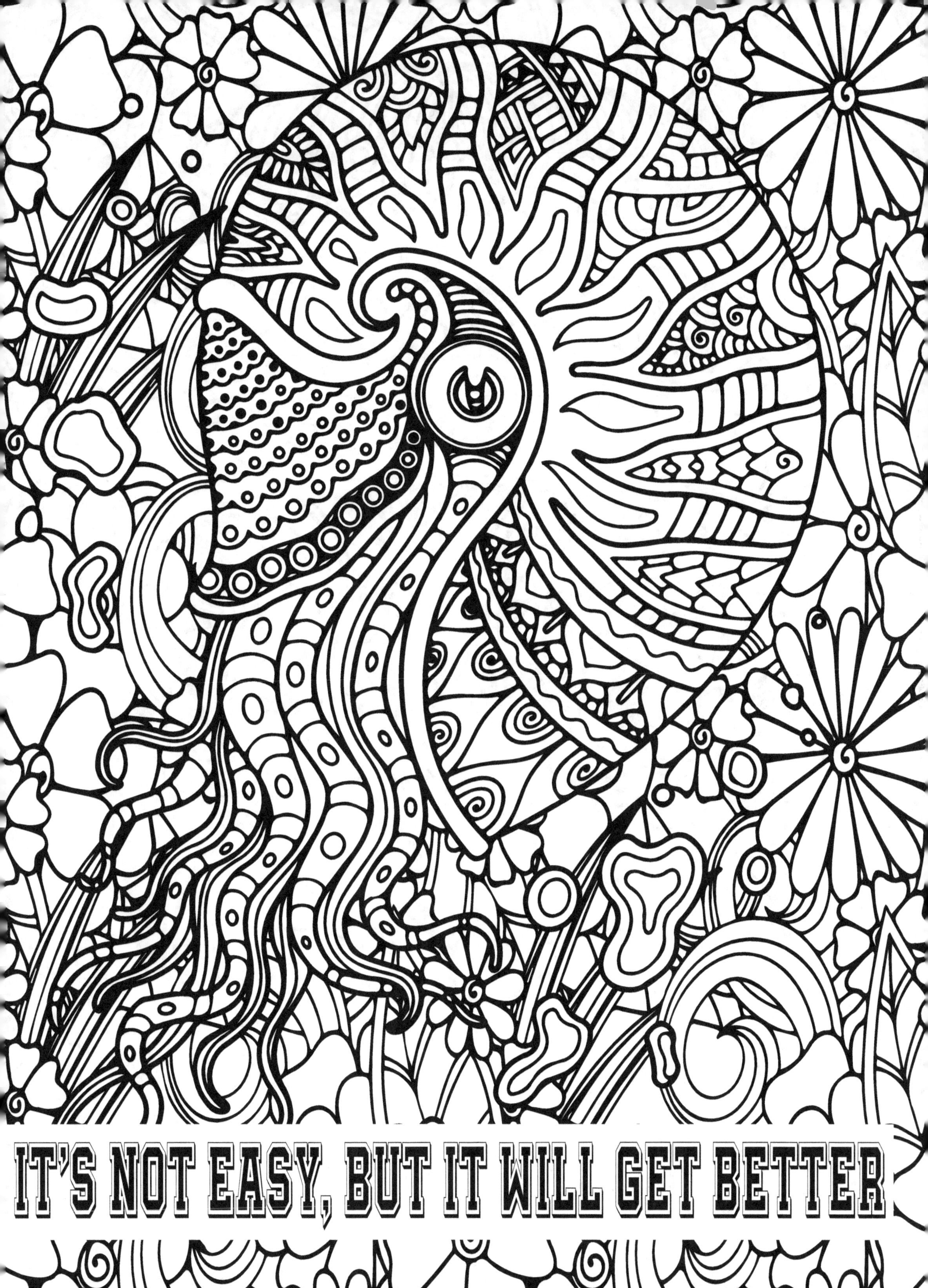
IT'S NOT EASY, BUT IT WILL GET BETTER

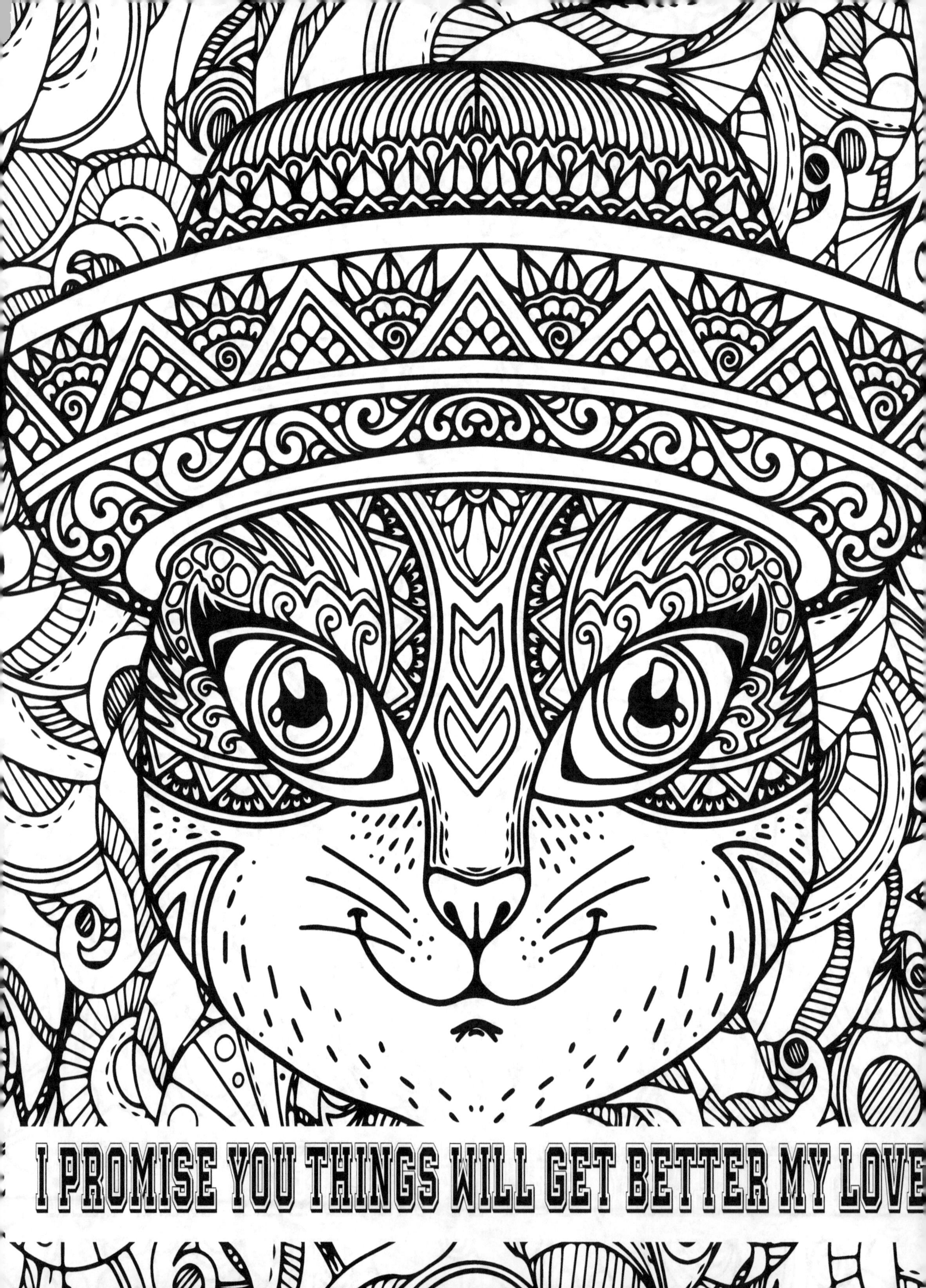
I PROMISE YOU THINGS WILL GET BETTER MY LOVE

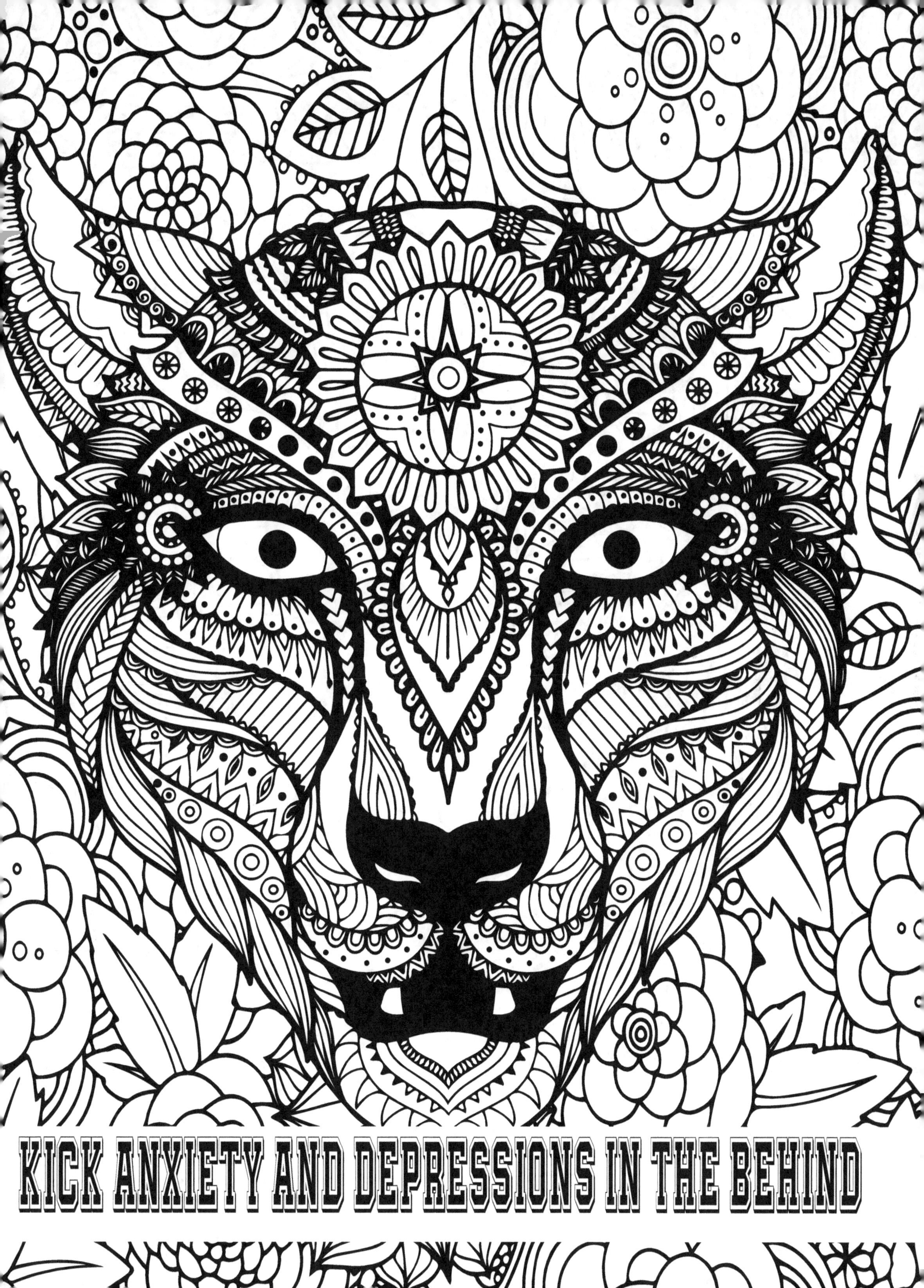
KICK ANXIETY AND DEPRESSIONS IN THE BEHIND

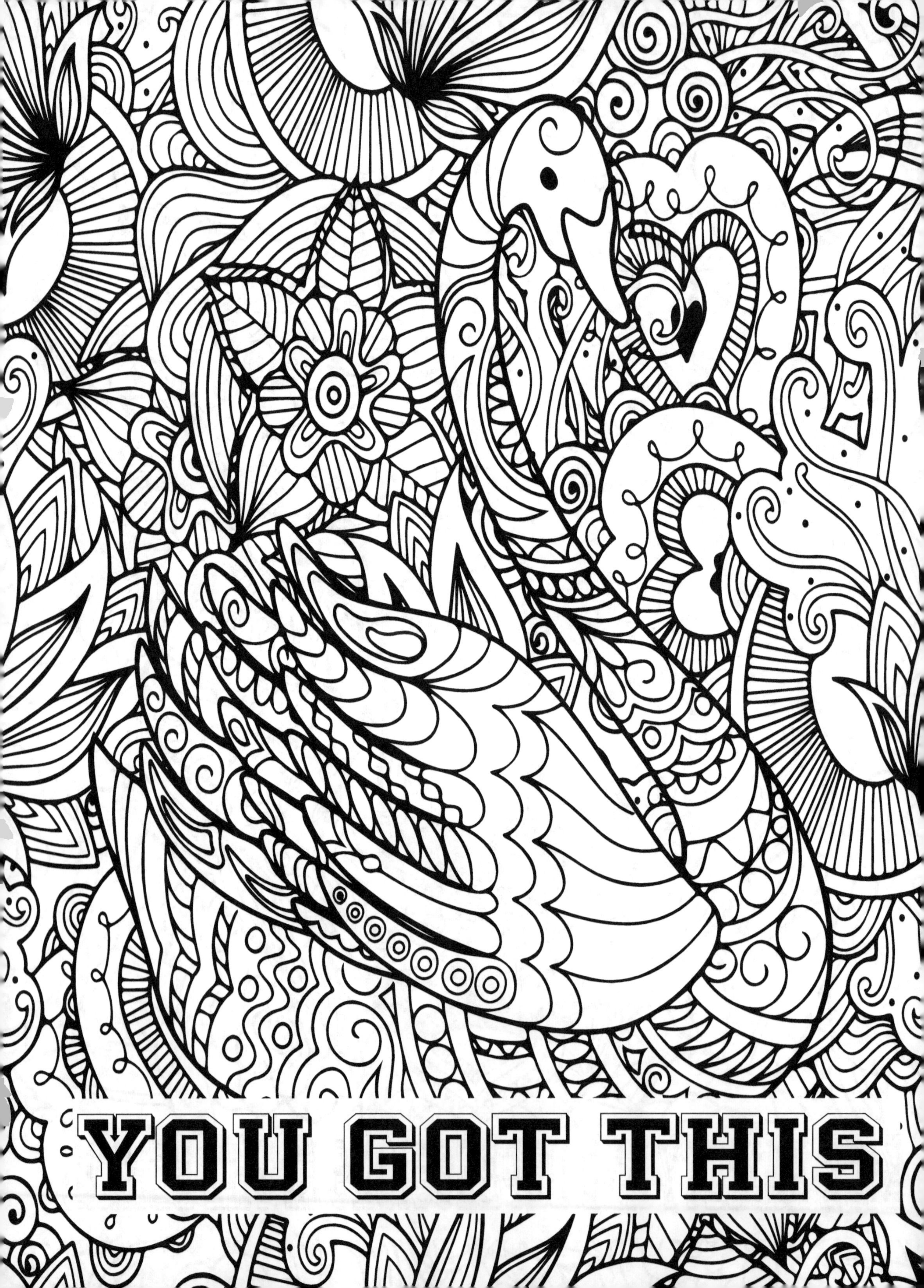
YOU GOT THIS

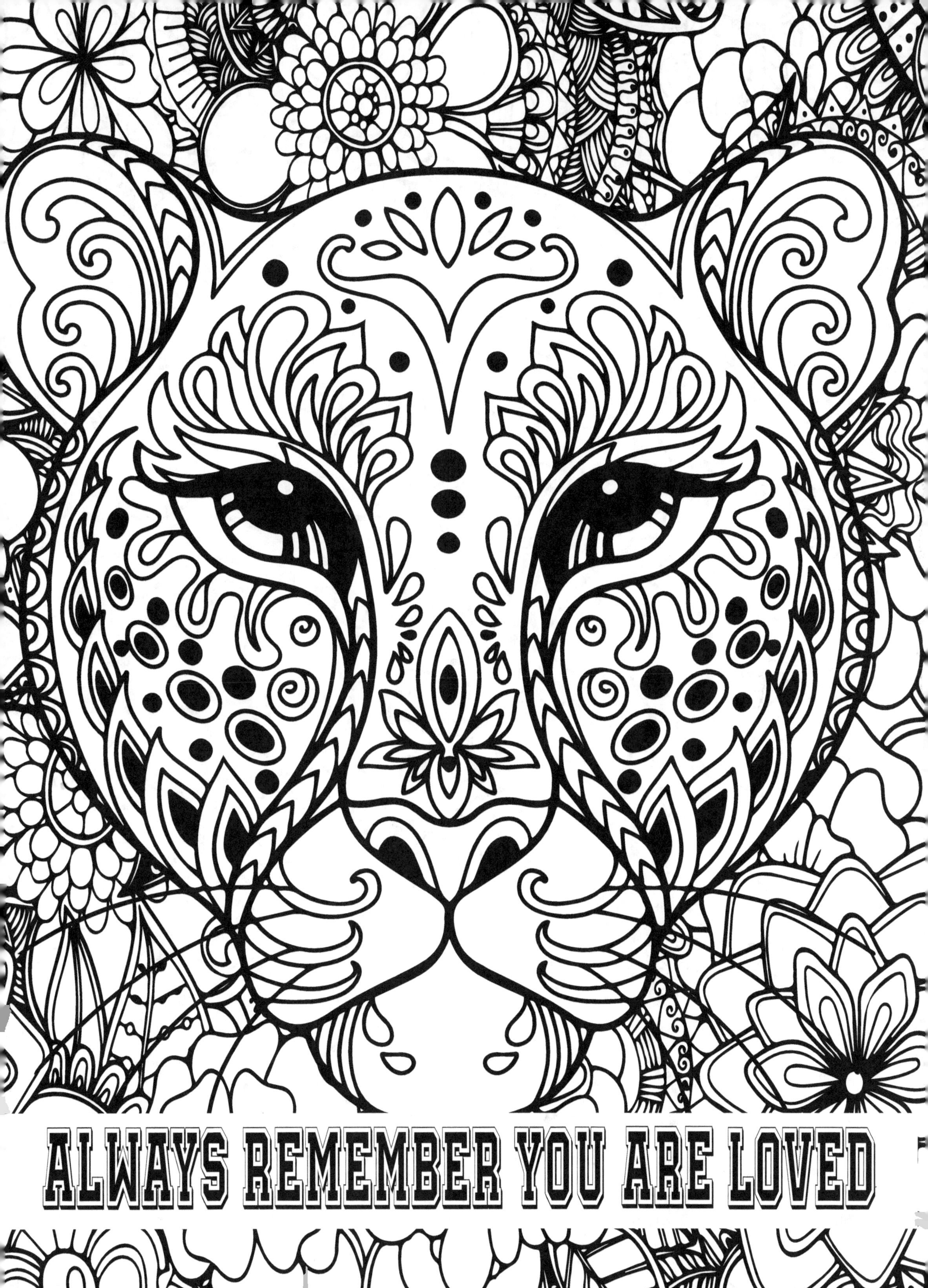
ALWAYS REMEMBER YOU ARE LOVED

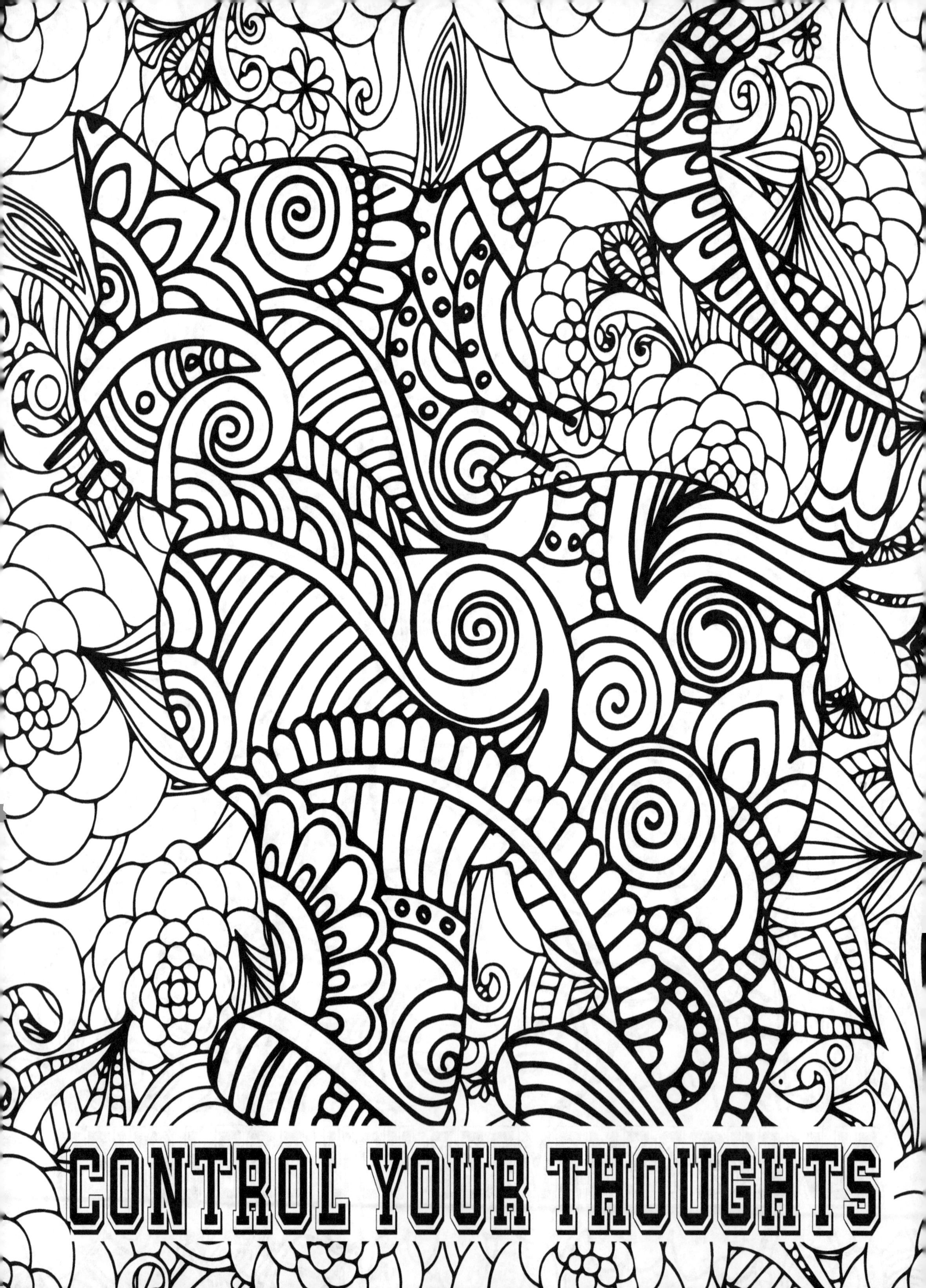
CONTROL YOUR THOUGHTS

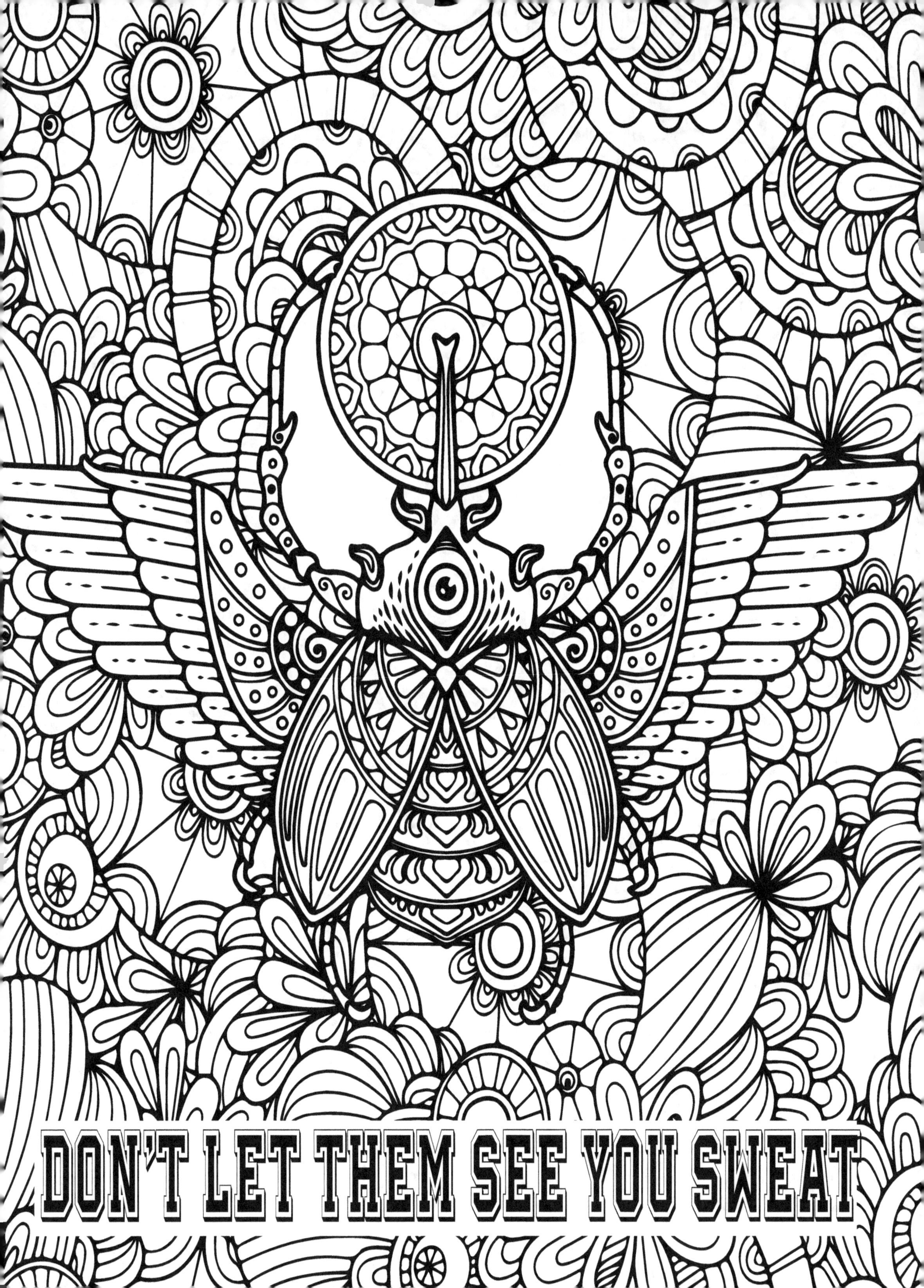
DON'T LET THEM SEE YOU SWEAT

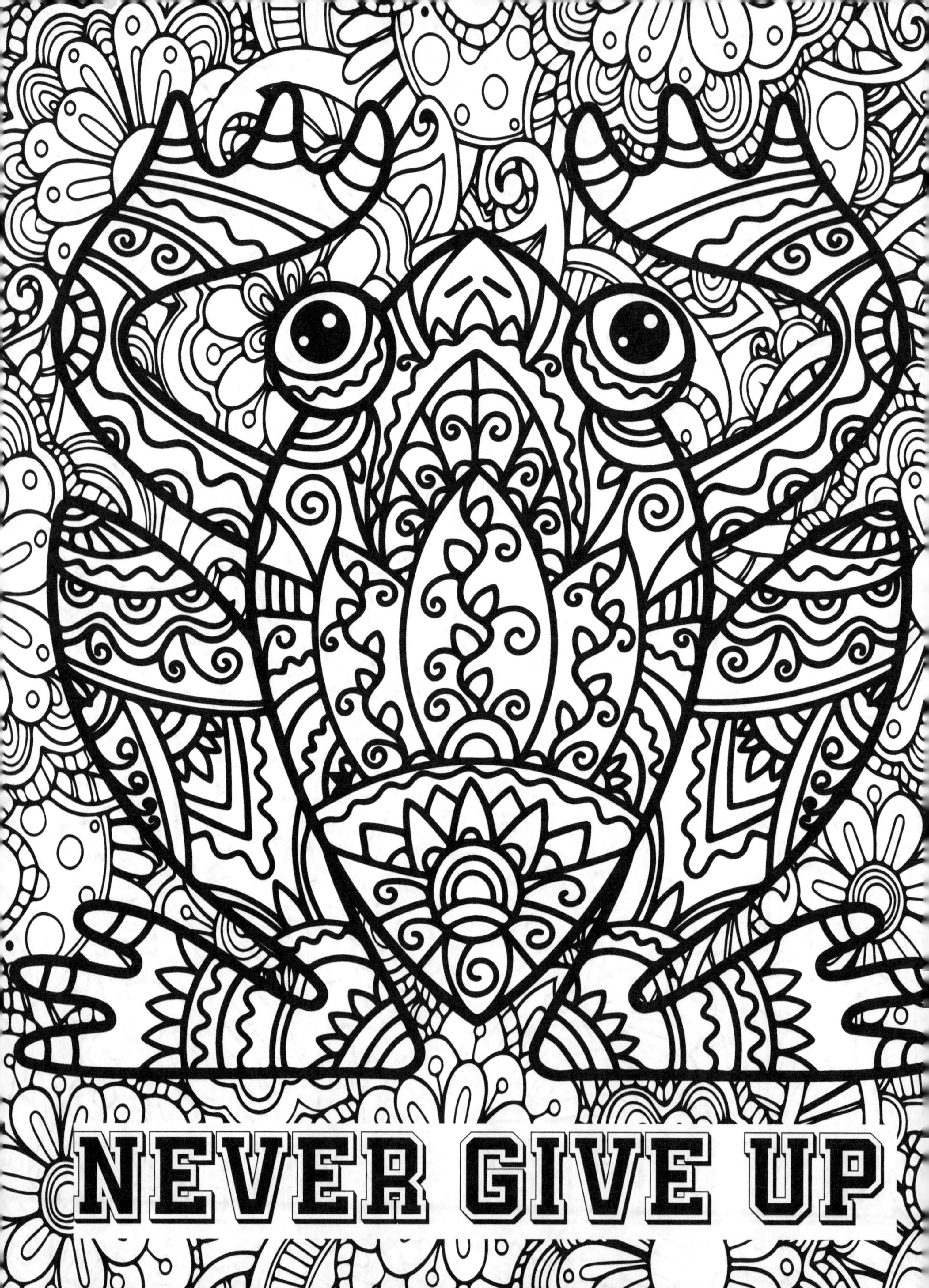
NEVER GIVE UP

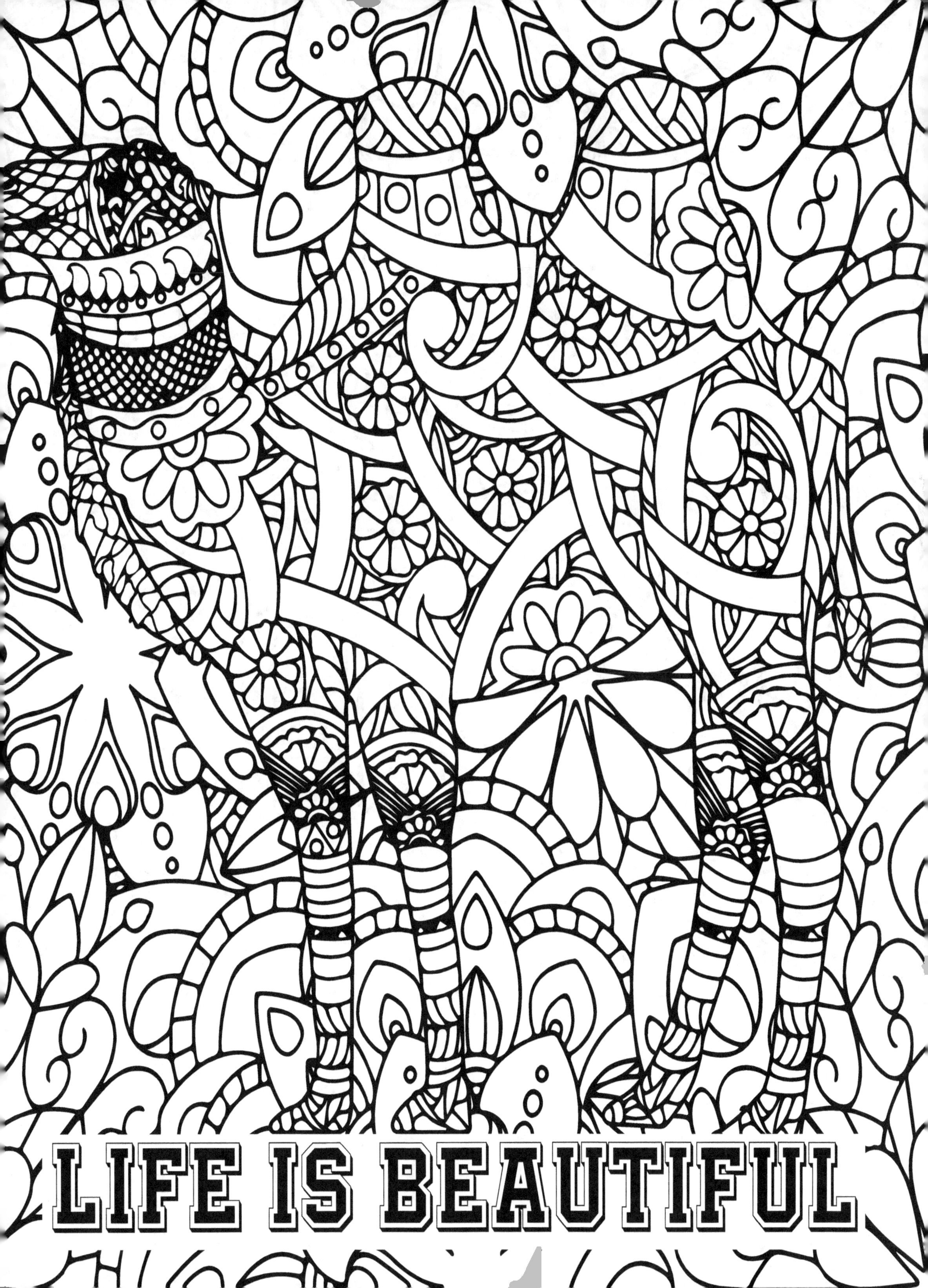
LIFE IS BEAUTIFUL

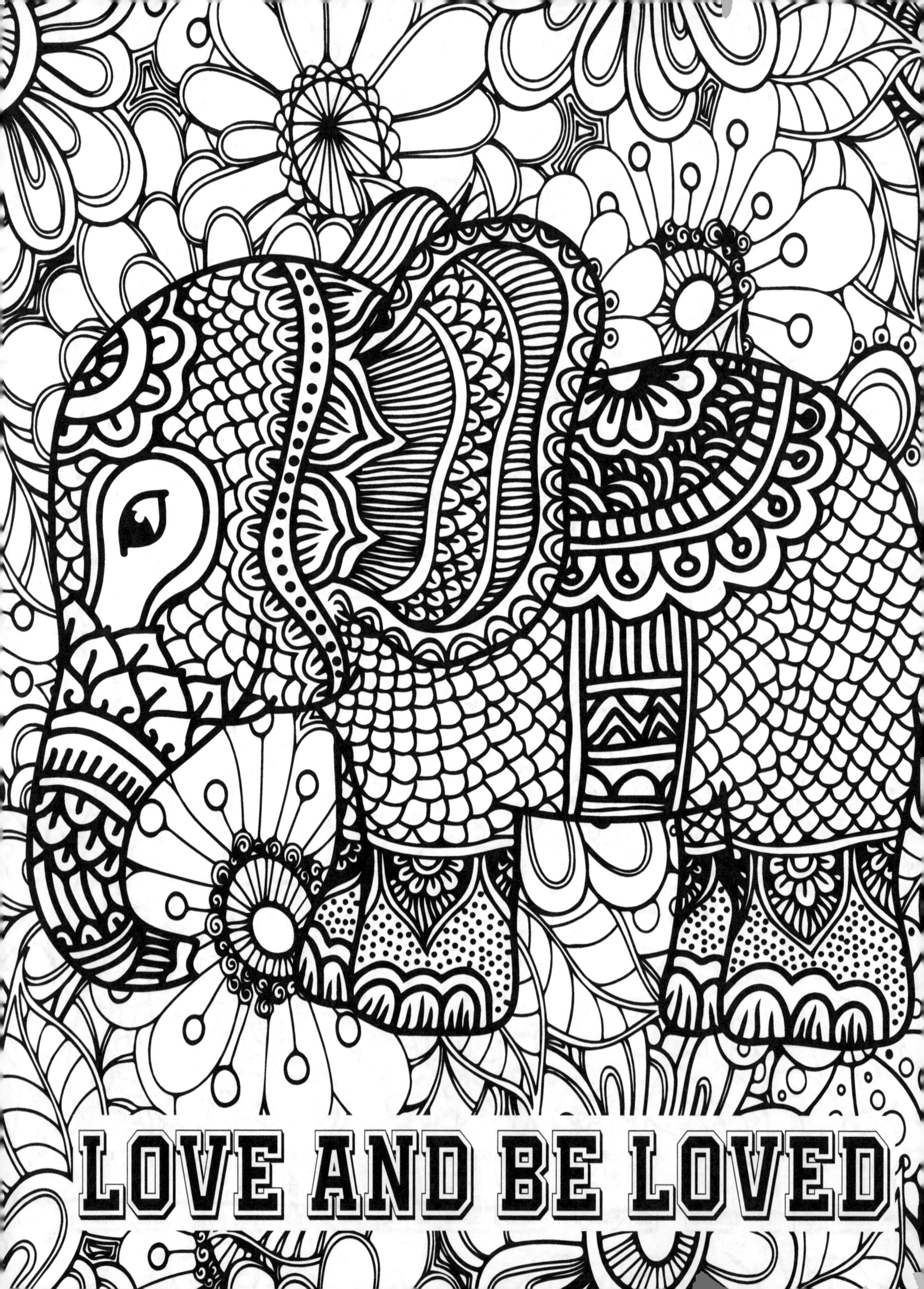
LOVE AND BE LOVED

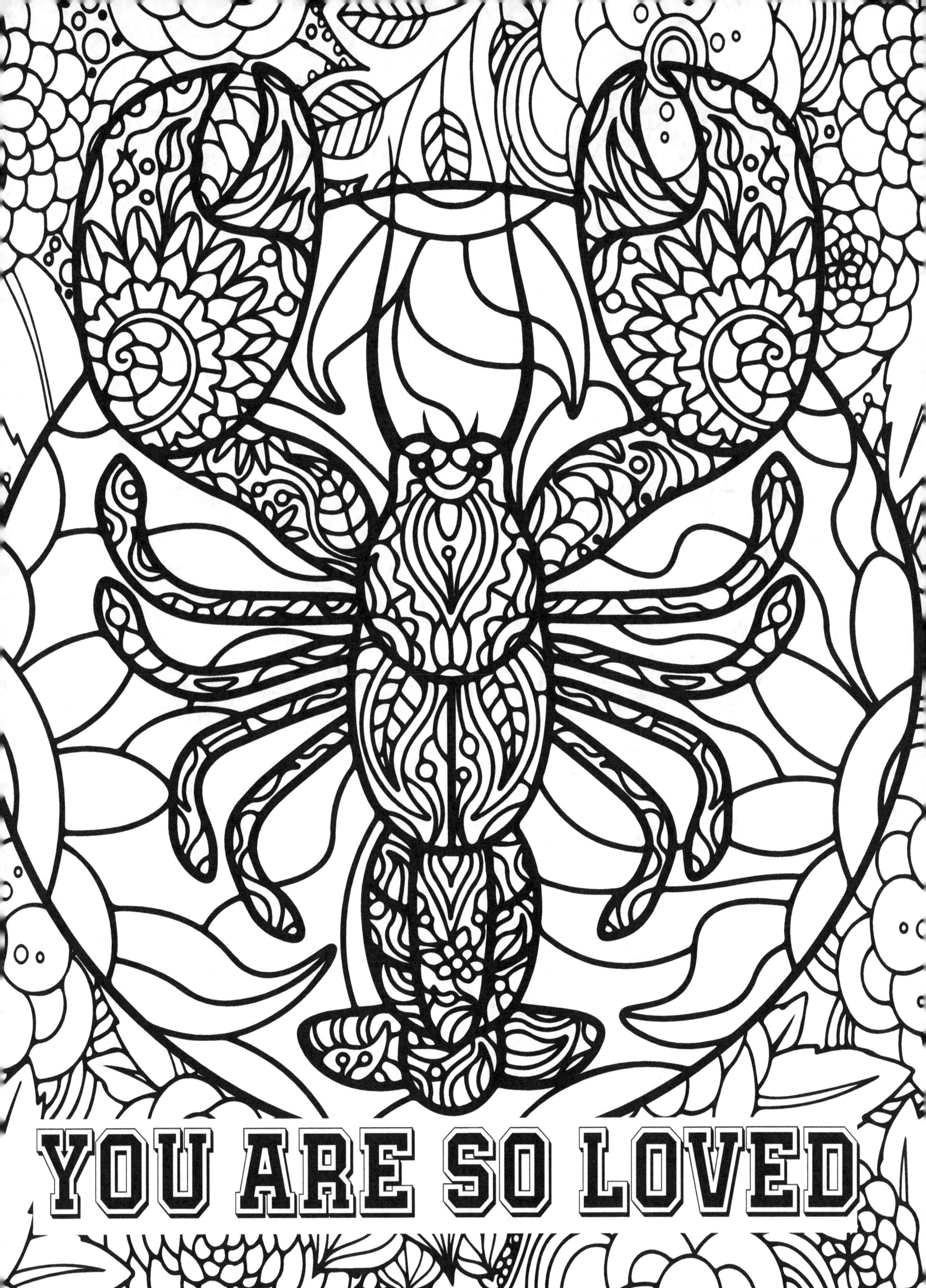
YOU ARE SO LOVED

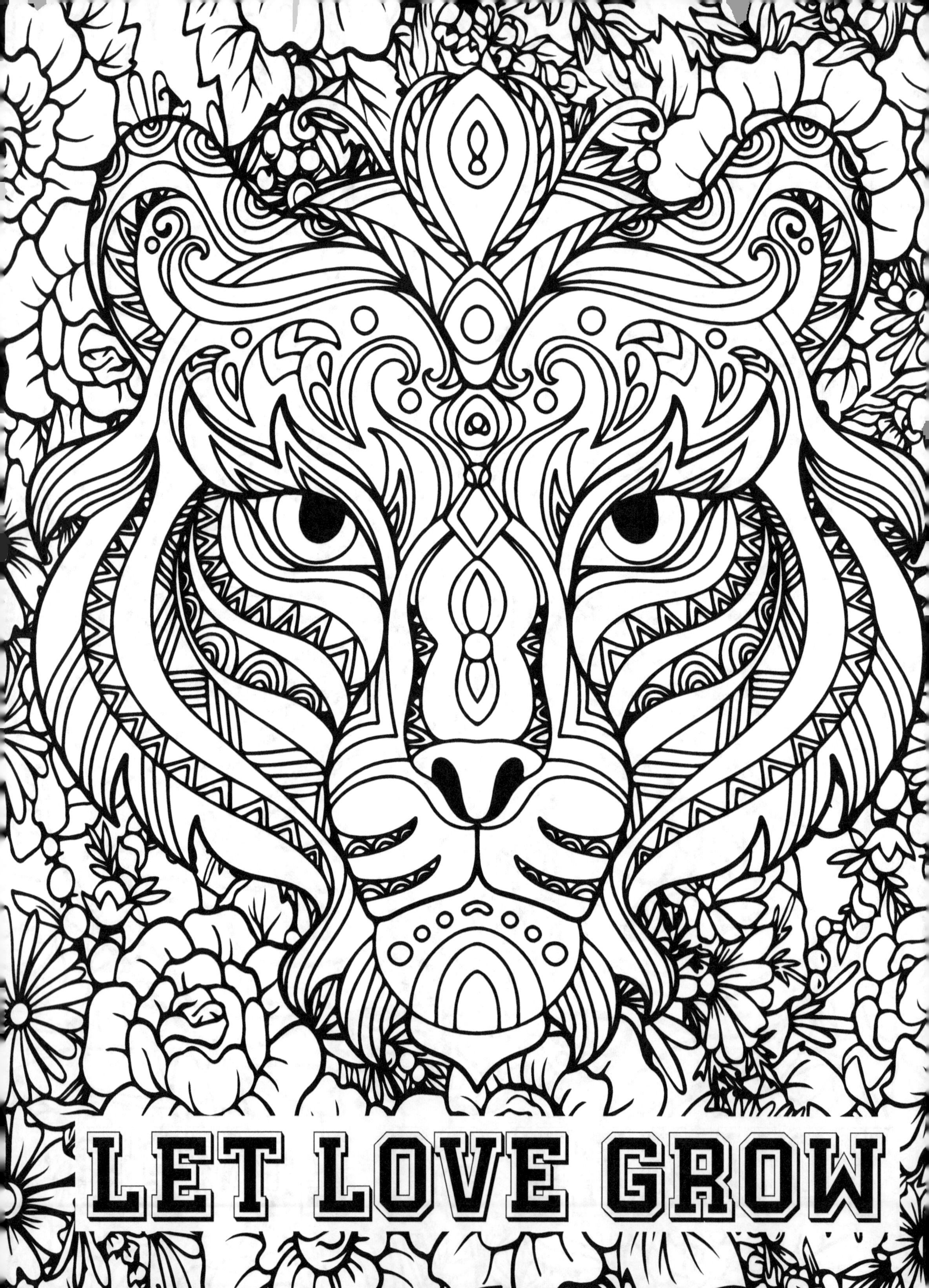
LET LOVE GROW

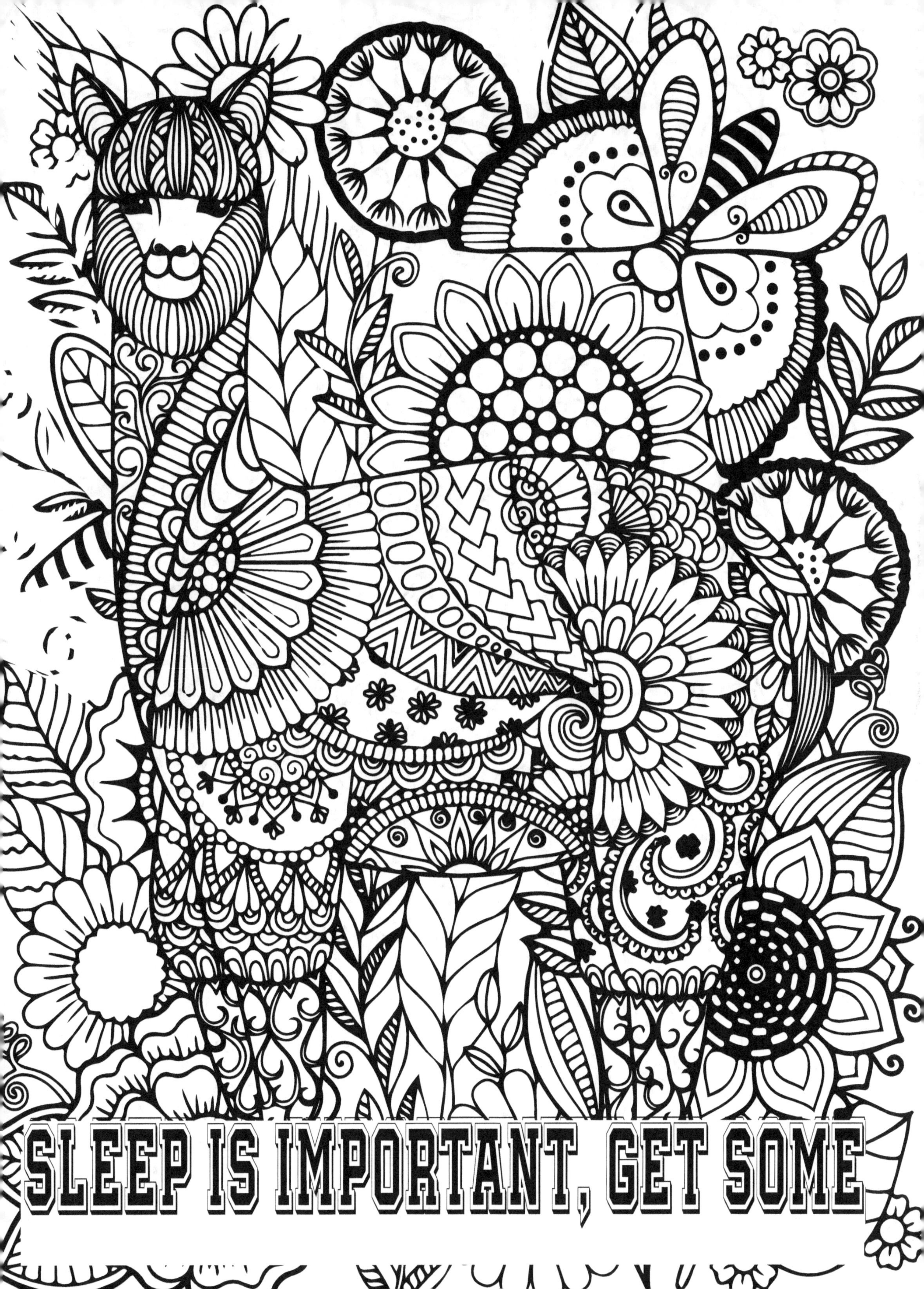
SLEEP IS IMPORTANT, GET SOME

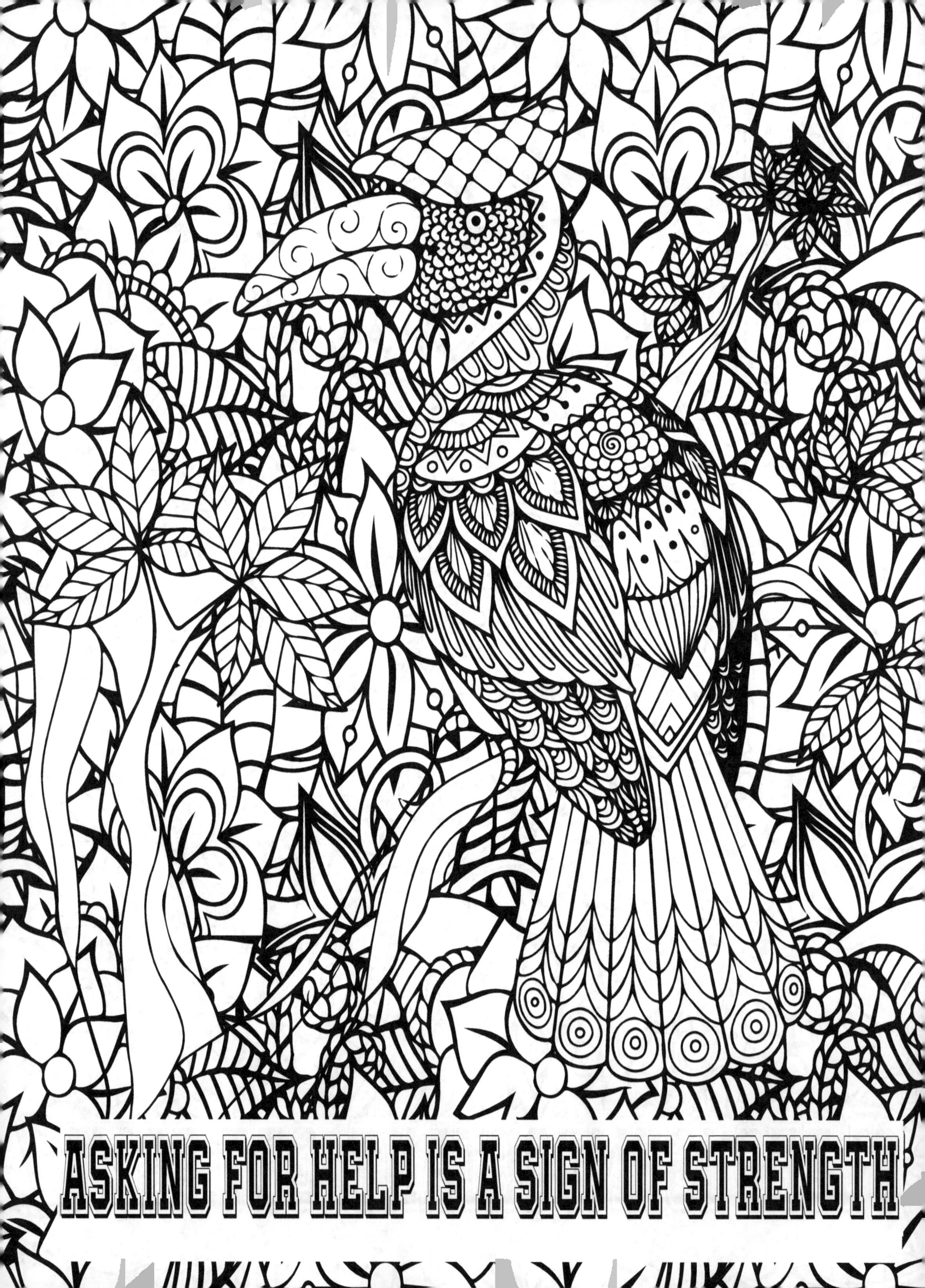
ASKING FOR HELP IS A SIGN OF STRENGTH

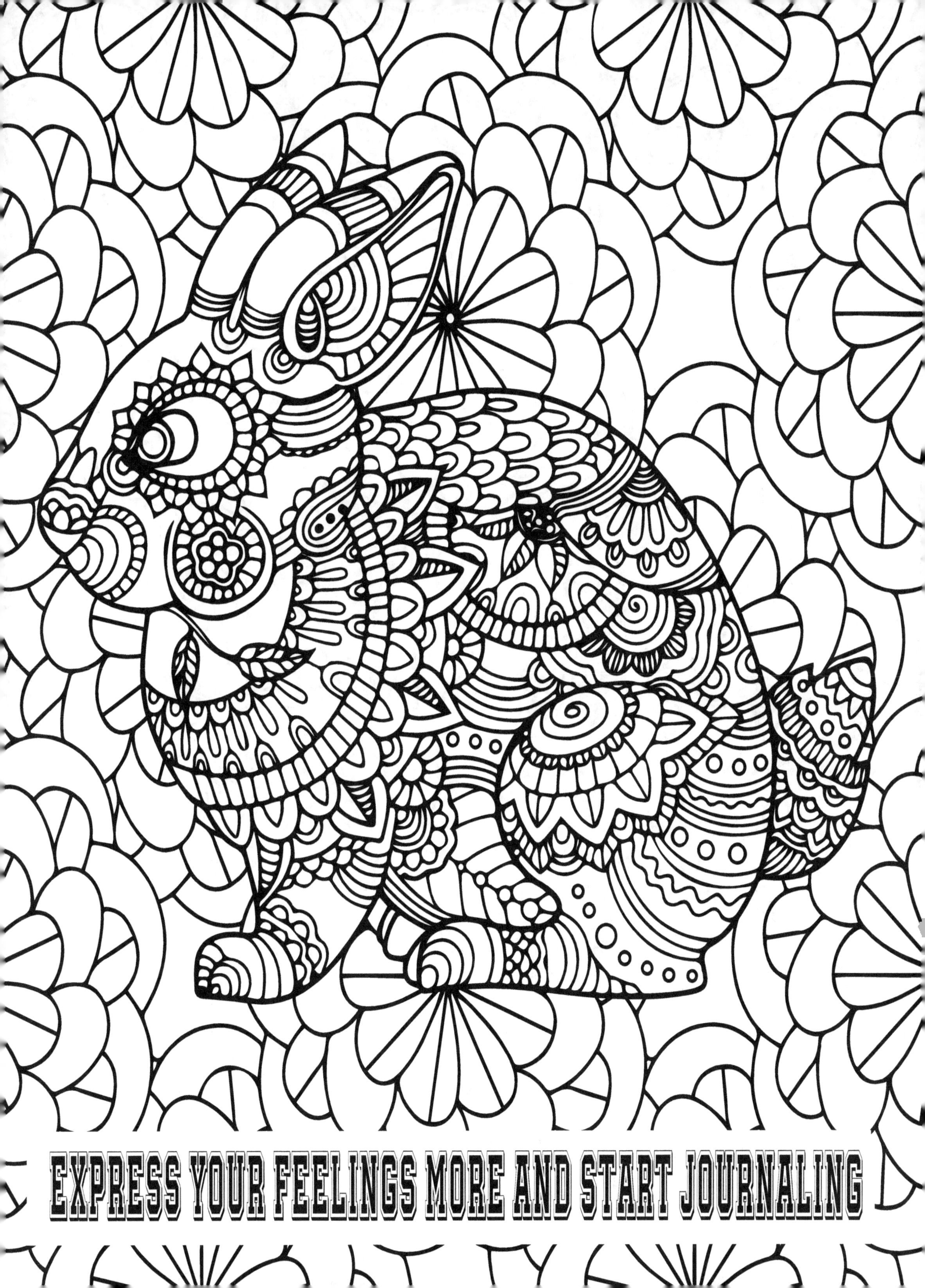
EXPRESS YOUR FEELINGS MORE AND START JOURNALING

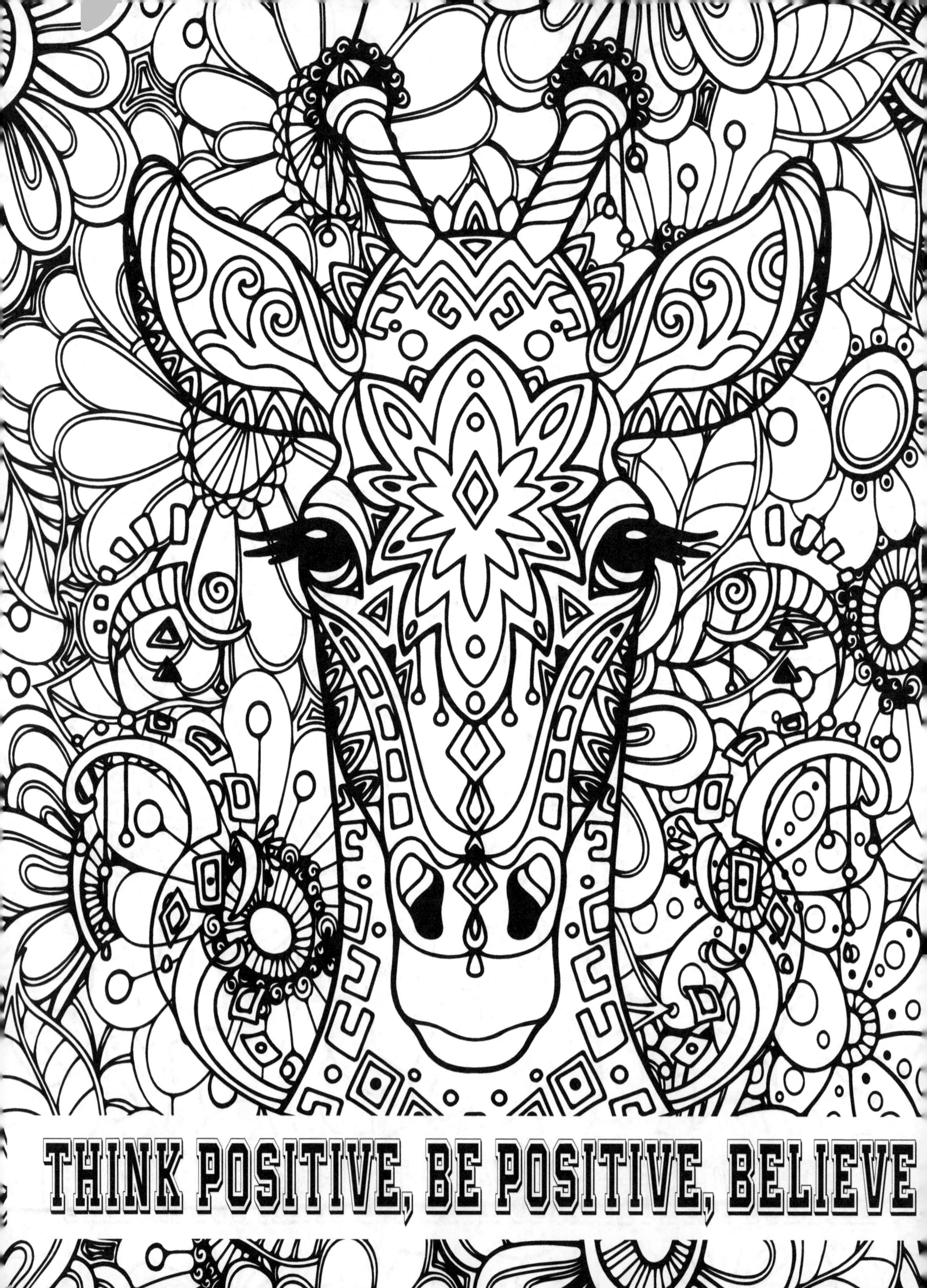
THINK POSITIVE, BE POSITIVE, BELIEVE

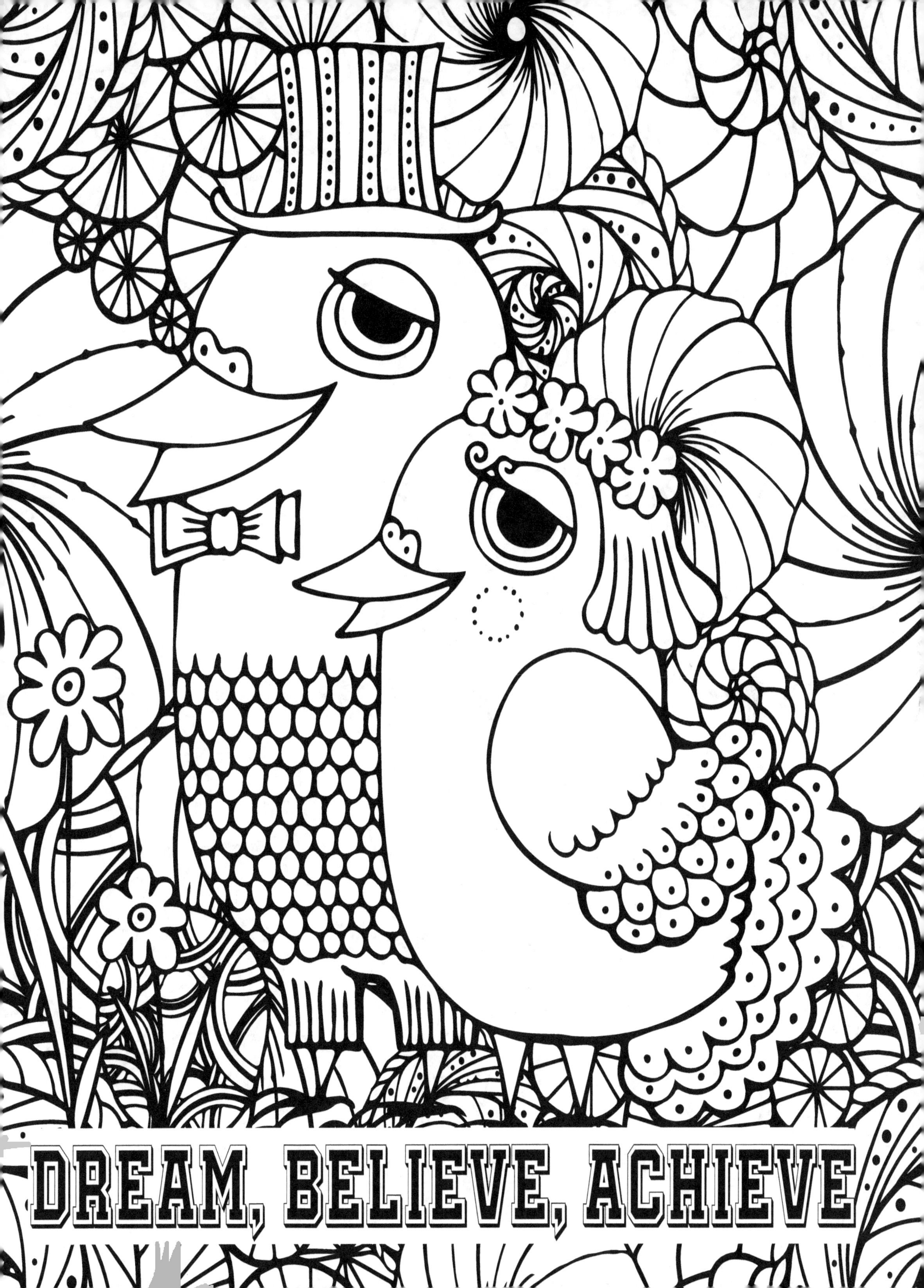
DREAM, BELIEVE, ACHIEVE

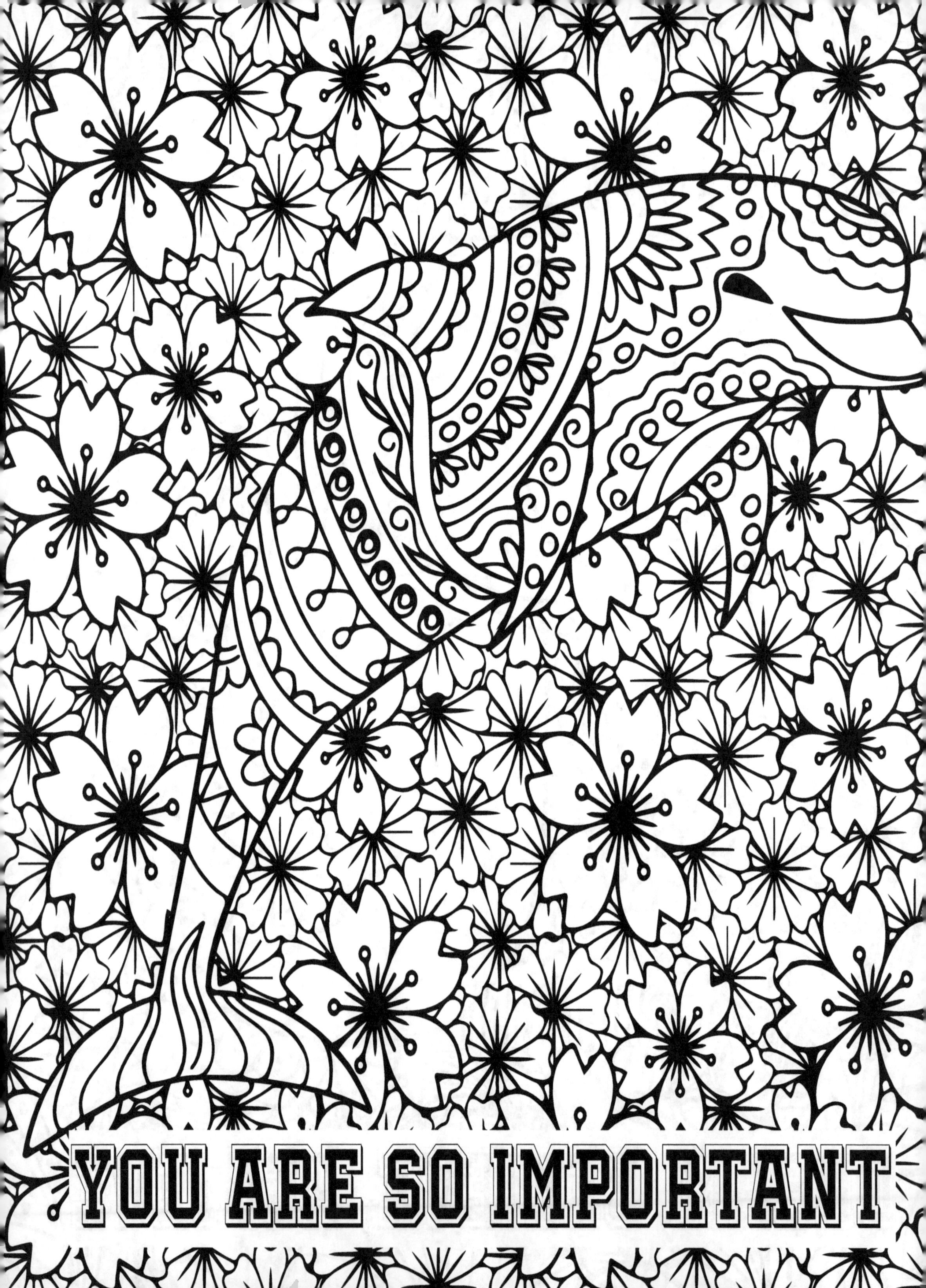
YOU ARE SO IMPORTANT

www.ingramcontent.com/pod-product-compliance
Lightning Source LLC
LaVergne TN
LVHW061257100826
845148LV00008B/1160

* 9 7 8 1 7 3 6 3 5 9 1 6 7 *